For my mother and first teacher, Edvige Orsini Galli
and in memory of my father, Valentino Galli

THE
IL FORNAIO
Baking Book

*Sweet and Savory
Recipes from
the Italian Kitchen*

BY FRANCO GALLI

CHRONICLE BOOKS
SAN FRANCISCO

A hardcover edition of this book was originally published in 1993 by Chronicle Books LLC.

Copyright © 1993 by Il Fornaio America Corporation

Library of Congress Cataloging-in-Publication Data:

Galli, Franco.
The Il Fornaio baking book: sweet and savory recipes from the Italian kitchen / by Franco Galli

*   p.   cm.*
Includes index.
ISBN 0-8118-3297-X
1. Baking — Italy
2. Cookery, Italian.
3. Bread — Italy.
4. Fornaio.   I. Title.
TX 765.G27   1993
641.7'1 — dc20
92-21533 CIP

Photography by Daniel Proctor

Printed in Hong Kong

Distributed in Canada by Raincoast Books
9050 Shaughnessy Street
Vancouver, BC V6P 6E5

10 9 8 7 6 5 4 3 2

Chronicle Books LLC
85 Second Street
San Francisco, CA 94105

www.chroniclebooks.com

TABLE OF CONTENTS

INTRODUCTION

Italians have given the world the sculptures of Michelangelo, the operas of Verdi, the poetry of Dante, the scientific discoveries of Galileo, the political philosophy of Machiavelli. When our thoughts turned to daily life, we also came up with the radio, Venetian blinds, Parmesan cheese, Bolognese sauce, and, of course, a matchless wealth of breads and sweets. We are proud of our rich heritage and are also very protective of it.

I was born at the end of World War II in the small Lombardian town of Carpenedolo, not far from Brescia. Most Italians then still shopped at a neighborhood *panificio,* where the baker — *il fornaio* — worked long hours preparing breads unique to the region. Some customers even paid a small fee to secure space in the bakeries' great brick-lined ovens for their own hand-shaped loaves.

In the mid-1950s, my grandfather found me a job at the Panificio d'Alba, which stood in Carpenedolo's main piazza and was the biggest and best bakery in town. I went to work at five in the morning and helped make bread until half-past ten. Then I would load my bicycle with loaves hot from the charcoal-fired *forno* and deliver them to farm families in the nearby countryside. In the afternoon I concentrated on preparing tarts, cakes, and other sweets. I was particularly adept at making *le pesche;* each "peach" was formed from two pieces of sweet dough that had been brushed with a reddish liqueur and lemon juice, sprinkled with crystal sugar, and joined with a jam filling. I made only a little money, but could take home as much bread to my family as I could carry.

In these same years two mighty forces, the move toward large-scale bakery operations and the mechanization of agriculture, began to threaten not only such shops as the Panificio d'Alba, but Italy's entire baking legacy. It was a time when wood-fired ovens were giving way to gas ones, and fields once sown with ancient wheat strains were planted with more productive hybrid varieties. Indeed, Lombardy, with its superior soil, temperate climate, and industrious farmers, was destined to be Italy's most agriculturally advanced region, eventually boasting, among other claims, the country's largest wheat yields per acre.

But such progress always comes at a cost. The price to Italians may well have been the potential loss of a culinary tradition that reaches back to the glory days of ancient Rome, when bakers were among the empire's wealthiest, most respected citizens. Archaeological excavations of a bakery oven at Pompeii have uncovered more than eighty loaves of wheat bread, culinary artifacts retrieved from that cataclysmic August day in A.D. 79, when Mount Vesuvius buried the city. These loaves are remarkably similar to the breads eaten in southern Italy today, nineteen centuries later.

It is this extraordinary baking heritage that another Lombardian family, the Veggettis of Milan, set out to preserve in the early 1970s. For many years they had been in the business of designing bakery interiors. And as "modernization" fever struck Italy, they did not like what they saw developing in their own industry.

The art of Italian baking was in danger. The loaves of insipid, cottony white bread and bags of indifferent *biscotti* being turned out by industrial-sized bakeries were pushing to become the Italian standards. Instead of accepting fate, the Veggetti family decided to do something about it. They gathered authentic regional recipes, searched out bakers who knew the traditional ways of preparing them, and opened a school to teach young students how to make the same breads and *dolci* that had sustained their ancestors. Then they launched the now-famous chain of Il Fornaio bakeries — presently numbering more than fifteen hundred throughout Europe — with an absolute determination to bake the best way: the old way. Since its inception, Il Fornaio has used only the finest and purest ingredients available, and every bread and dessert it offers is formed by hand and sold fresh daily.

In 1980, Il Fornaio America, adopting the same attention to detail and integrity of ingredients as their Milanese associates, was established in the United States. Initially we were just one small shop in San Francisco, but it was soon followed with branches throughout California. Today our name appears not only on bakeries, but on restaurants and cafes as well.

When I joined Il Fornaio America, my assignment was to oversee the preparation of the traditional foods of Italy in both the bakeries and the restaurants. Many years had passed since my days at the Panificio d'Alba, but I have always had deeply affectionate memories of that time. It was a chance to return to the world of powdery flour sacks and richly fermenting yeast, crusty brown loaves and delicate jam tarts — the warm, ancient world of my youth, a wonderful legacy to preserve for the future. Now, in this, Il Fornaio's first cookbook, I hope to bring some of that same legacy to you.

Readers who are also Il Fornaio bakery customers will find old friends in these pages, a full array of easy-to-use recipes for your favorite breads, rolls, pizzas, cookies, cakes, and tarts. Those who have never been to our bakeries will discover the ability to produce a cornucopia of authentic Italian breads and sweets in their own kitchens.

I have included directions for making such regional specialties as *ciabatta*, the large, chewy, slipper-shaped loaf native to the Lake Como region; *focaccia alla genovese*, the Ligurian flat bread that is a descendant of the ancient *fougasse* of French Provence; the appealingly crunchy *cantucci di Prato*, Tuscan *biscotti* that taste best when dipped into a glass of sweet Vin Santo; *colomba pasquale*, the Lombardian Easter bread shaped like a dove and studded with candied orange rind; and *tiramisù*, the espresso-laced Venetian dessert that has gone international. There is also a chapter on what to do with leftover bread that goes far beyond the usual suggestions of crumbs and croutons.

Throughout the book, there are stories I heard as a boy, little fables I hope will entertain you with the colorful history and lore that surrounds Italian baking. You will learn how *panettone* was given a bulbous top to celebrate the domes of Lombardy's great cathedrals. Why the Tuscans do not put any salt in their *pane toscano*. How the Sicilian respect for bread will not allow a loaf to be cut before it is anointed with the sign of the cross. How the town of Saronno has become world famous for its *amaretti*, chewy macaroons flavored with almonds.

There is information on equipment, ingredients, and techniques — everything you will need to bake Il Fornaio's famed breads and sweets at home. I have deliberately developed recipes that can be made without expensive equipment and that call for few special ingredients. The most exotic tools you will find in these pages are a baker's peel — the wooden paddle we use to slide breads into the oven — and a baking stone; but even they can be replaced by an ordinary sheet pan. If you have a heavy-duty mixer with assorted bread-making attachments or a food processor, fine. But you do not need either one. As my American-born children would say, these are "low-tech" breads and sweets. Handmade, beautiful, and delicious.

It is my wish that this book will both instruct and intrigue you, that in it I have passed along the same infectious spirit for Italian baking that I feel whenever I myself begin to knead the dough for a loaf of crusty *pagnotta* or to shape the pastry for a *crostata di frutta fresca.*

❖　❖　❖

LA PANETTERIA DEL FORNAIO

The Baker's Kitchen

EQUIPMENT

The baking of breads and sweets is an ancient art that long predates the food processor, heavy-duty stationary mixer, and electric convection oven. Put simply, you do not need a kitchenful of exotic equipment to bake glorious breads and enticing sweets.

Because this is a book of free-form breads shaped by hand, you do not even need bread pans. You do need bowls, measuring cups and spoons for wet and dry ingredients, good knives, whisks and sturdy wooden spoons, and an oven that you know well. Other necessary equipment is discussed here. All of it can be found in kitchen shops, gourmet catalogs, or the cookware sections of department stores. Any other equipment is more or less a frill.

BAKER'S PEEL   The Il Fornaio bakerman is never seen without one of these smooth wooden paddles in his hand. A baker's peel is the best way to slide breads, rolls, and pizzas into a hot oven, and, because of its beveled edge, the best way to retrieve them. Peels sold for the home kitchen are usually made of basswood or alderwood, come in various sizes, up to about eighteen inches by sixteen inches, and have handles about eight inches long. If you consider the peel a frill, transport your loaves on a cornmeal-dusted baking sheet without sides.

BAKING SHEET   If you do not have a baking stone, heavy-gauge baking sheets of black carbon steel are ideal for baking most breads. Heavy-weight aluminum is recommended for *biscotti* and delicate loaves, such as *challah*. Buy the best; inexpensive sheets warp in high heat.

BAKING STONE   Baking breads and pizzas on a porous unglazed stone gives them wonderful crisp crusts that baking on sheet pans cannot match. The flat stones, which distribute heat exceptionally evenly, are either round or rectangular and come in different sizes; the bigger, the better, but measure your oven before you shop. Unglazed quarry tiles (look for them in a shop selling floor tiles) can be used, too. Buy enough of these square tiles to line the floor of a gas oven (avoid covering any vent holes) or the lowest rack of an electric oven completely; you may need to have some trimmed to fit.

Above the left shoulder of the Il Fornaio bakerman is the outline of a stone oven, which illustrates that baking on stone is basic to our recipes. If you lack a stone, bake your breads and pizzas on cornmeal-dusted or parchment paper–lined baking sheets.

Dough can be left to rise in a vessel of almost any shape made from almost any material, except perhaps untreated steel or iron, which might impart an off-taste. Indeed, a ball of dough left on the floor will rise — although certainly not to great height. I specify square dishes in a few of the recipes because I want the dough to rise in that particular shape for ease in forming loaves. In these cases, porcelain or ceramic is my preference, but a metal pan would do as well. Put simply, selecting a vessel in which to place dough for rising is a question of aesthetics and personal taste and not of rigid rules.

CAKE AND TART PANS   The cake and tart recipes call only for standard pans. But as with all the equipment in the baker's kitchen, quality is critical. Select heavy-gauge aluminum cake pans and loaf pans and tinned steel tube pans, springform pans, and fluted tart pans with removable bottoms.

Aluminum or ceramic pie weights are advised for prebaking unfilled tart shells. Even though many bakers believe that rice or beans work just as well, I find that they begin to smell when hot. And they do not smell like something you want in a tart.

COOKIE CUTTERS   Select heavy-gauge tinned steel cutters, plain and fluted, in graduated sizes. Cookware shops sell sets of cutters that include the most commonly needed sizes.

COOLING RACK   The most important thing about racks is that they be level and that you have enough of them to accommodate whatever you need to cool at one time, whether it be five dozen *biscotti* or two dozen *panini*.

DOUGH SCRAPERS   There are two types of dough scrapers. One is a rectangular steel-bladed scraper with a wooden or plastic handle for cutting dough and "scraping" work surfaces clean. The other is a rounded plastic scraper for scooping every last bit of dough out of bowls. Both are inexpensive and both are infinitely handy.

HAND-HELD MIXER   A lightweight hand-held mixer with at least three speeds is a workhorse for the sweets baker. It is practical for creaming butter and sugar, beating egg whites and cream, whipping eggs and sugar to the ribbon stage, and mixing soft doughs.

PARCHMENT PAPER   Kitchen parchment is invaluable for lining baking pans for cookies and cakes and some breads. It does not tear when wet and can withstand very high oven temperatures. It is also reusable, which makes it an economical buy. Silicone-treated parchment is best for baking because it is stick resistant. Look for rolls of parchment in the finest cookware shops, through gourmet catalogs, or in restaurant and baking supply stores. If you cannot find parchment, grease the pans with butter.

PASTRY BAG   Pastry bags are generally used for piping decorations onto fanciful *torte* and for forming certain *biscotti*. A good-sized pastry bag, preferably with a plastic lining, and a simple assortment of plain and star tips are all you need.

ROLLING PIN   I like a heavy rolling pin, so that the pin does most of the work. It should be about fifteen inches long and made of heavy hardwood, with ball bearing–loaded handles.

SCALE   Kitchen scales for weighing ingredients are available in three main types: spring, balance, and electronic. Spring models are quick to use, but their spring mechanisms lose tautness and thus accuracy over time. Balance scales, which require the adjusting of weights by hand along a beam, are dependably accurate. Battery-operated electronic scales are very precise, but also very pricy.

SPRAY MISTER   Misting breads headed for the oven and the hot oven itself ensures richly colored, crisp crusts. Any mister that releases a fine spray of water is ideal.

THERMOMETERS   An instant-read thermometer is the best way to test for water temperature when dissolving yeast. A candy thermometer is useful for checking the temperature of sugar syrups. An oven thermometer lets you know if the oven dial setting matches the true internal temperature of the oven. (If it does not, adjust the dial and wait for the oven to reach the correct temperature before you begin baking.)

WORK SURFACE   A wooden board is fine for working with both bread dough and cookie and pastry doughs. On hot days, a marble surface keeps pastry doughs cool. But almost any clean, firm, even surface of comfortable height can be used for such tasks, from a Formica countertop to a wooden tabletop.

◆ ◆ ◆

INGREDIENTS

Bakers need only a handful of ingredients to make bread: yeast, water, flour, and salt. Italy's seemingly countless breads are the result of varying the amounts of these ingredients, the number of risings, the sizes and shapes of the loaves, and the temperature of the oven. Some loaves are further embellished with nuts or fruits; others are dotted with herbs or punctuated with salty olives. In every case, however, such ingredients should be of the highest quality.

Ingredients for cookies and desserts demand the same attention to quality. Settle for nothing less than the best chocolate for your Turinese torte and the freshest sweet butter for your flaky pastry shells.

BUTTER   Unsalted butter has a delicate, sweet flavor that is preferred for baking both breads and desserts.

CANDIED FRUITS AND FRUIT RINDS
Many different types of fruits and fruit rinds are cooked in sugar syrup and then dried and sold in candied form. The Italians are experts at preparing these sugary morsels for use in everything from *panettone* to *panforte.* Purchase only the best-quality candied fruits and fruit rinds; avoid those that are prepared with artificial colors and preservatives.

CHOCOLATE   Buy the finest chocolate – bittersweet, semisweet, sweet – your pocketbook can afford; imported Italian and Swiss brands such as Perugina and Callebaut are recommended. White chocolate, which is not classified as true chocolate in the United States because it lacks

chocolate liquor, should be selected with the same eye to quality.

Dutch-process unsweetened cocoa powder has been treated with alkali to intensify its color and temper its flavor. It is preferred over the nonalkalized cocoa powder commonly made in the United States, which has a more bitter taste.

EGGS   Except where noted, all of the recipes are based on fresh grade AA large eggs.

EXTRACTS   I have used only a handful of extracts in this book – almond, vanilla, lemon, anise. Pass over imitation-flavored extracts; the small cost difference for pure extracts is worth it.

FLOURS   Most of the bread recipes call for unbleached bread flour, a "strong" flour made from hard wheat that easily develops gluten, a protein substance that expands in a hot oven to give breads loft and volume. Some of the breads as well as most of the sweets call for unbleached all-purpose flour, a blend of soft-wheat and hard-wheat flours. Cake flour is milled exclusively from soft wheat and gives finished baked goods a crumbly quality. Whole-wheat flour is made from whole wheat kernels and produces a heavier, denser loaf or sweet.

Unprocessed wheat bran is the outside husk of the wheat berry removed during the initial stages of flour milling. Semolina, which is milled from the endosperm of the durum (hard) wheat berry and is available in various grinds, adds a creamy tint and chewy texture to breads. Medium-grind semolina, which is the easiest to find, can be used in breads.

Use medium-grind cornmeal for dusting the baker's peel. If you have bought fine-grind cornmeal for adding to breads or sweets, it will work on the peel as well. Nondegerminated cornmeal is best for baking, as it has more food value than cornmeal that has been stripped of the hull and germ in processing.

With the exception of bran, semolina, and nondegerminated cornmeal, which may require a trip to a health-food store or other specialty-food shop, all of these products are stocked in most supermarkets. In the case of every flour, shop where the inventory is frequently restocked.

LEAVENERS Fresh compressed yeast is used by most commercial bakers, but its perishability – it keeps for about two weeks under refrigeration – and lack of availability make it impractical for the home cook. Active dry yeast sold in small packets at most supermarkets or in bulk at health-food stores is an excellent alternative. Dry yeast can be stored in a cool, dry, dark cupboard for up to six months.

Readily available double-acting baking powder and baking soda are used to leaven cakes and cookies and some breads. Store them as you would dry yeast, replacing the container every six months.

NUTS Many Italian *biscotti* and *dolci* call for walnuts, almonds, and hazelnuts; the latter are especially popular in cakes and confections from the north. Delicate, pale ivory pine nuts are mixed into cookie doughs and sprinkled atop cakes.

Walnuts and almonds are carried in most supermarkets. Hazelnuts can be found in health-food stores, gourmet or Italian food shops, and in many supermarkets at holiday times. Pine nuts may also require a journey to a gourmet or Italian food shop. Because of their high oil content, nuts should be stored in tightly closed containers in a cool, dry place.

Almond paste, which is a dense mixture of ground blanched almonds and sugar, is sold in packages in gourmet shops and well-stocked supermarkets. Look for almond paste without preservatives or flavorings.

OLIVE OIL Olive oil makes breads wonderfully moist. At Il Fornaio we use imported extra-virgin olive oil in our breads because of its superior flavor. The best extra-virgin oil is cold-pressed without the aid of chemicals, is naturally low in acidity, and is quite costly. The first pressing of the olive produces a wonderfully fruity oil; try dipping bread into this deep green liquor for a delicious, low-cholesterol alternative to butter. Less-expensive chemically deacidified extra-virgin oils are also available. Olive oils produced from subsequent pressings, labeled simply "olive oil," are fine for oiling bowls or pans. We sell a high-quality extra-virgin olive oil under the Il Fornaio label in our shops.

SALT   Regular table salt can be added to bread doughs, but fine-grind sea salt is preferred because of its better, fresher flavor and slightly coarser texture. Coarse sea salt is used as a topping for some breads.

SUGAR   In addition to the usual granulated, brown, and powdered sugars, recipes call for crystal sugar, sometimes called coarse sugar or decorator's sugar, and amber turbinado sugar. Both are used as toppings and can be found in well-stocked supermarkets.

SEEDS   Italians add a variety of small seeds — fennel, anise, poppy, sesame — to their breads and *biscotti*. Sometimes they are mixed into the dough; sometimes they are simply scattered over the shaped loaf or cookies before baking.

Store seeds in tightly closed containers in a cool place. They lose their quality after about six months, so buy only what you can use within that time.

WINES AND LIQUEURS   Many Italian sweets are flavored with a wine or liqueur. I have called for a few such enhancements in these pages: the famous Sicilian Marsala wine, which comes in dry and sweet vintages; rum; and Amaretto (almond flavored), kirsch or maraschino (cherry flavored), and Frangelico (hazelnut flavored) liqueurs. Any well-stocked wine shop will carry these products.

◆ ◆ ◆

TECHNIQUES

Baking Breads

While the marketplace offers shiny heavy-duty mixers and sleek food processors for mixing and kneading dough, this is a book for people who want to bake bread the old-fashioned way. Making bread by hand is how you learn about bread, how you come to understand what it should feel like at each point in the process. It is the only way to know when the loaf is coming together successfully and when it is not.

ASSEMBLING THE INGREDIENTS   The first step is to read through the recipe carefully, then to assemble *all* of your ingredients at room temperature unless the recipe specifies otherwise. Cold ingredients will slow rising times. The next step is to dissolve the yeast in the amount of warm water specified in the recipe. The water must be about 105 degrees F, measured on an instant-read thermometer or by touch: it should feel pleasantly warm when poured over your wrist. Stir the yeast gently into the liquid and let it stand until it looks creamy, about 15 minutes.

MEASURING   Now measure the dry ingredients. Spoon them into cups or spoons and level the top with a knife blade; do not pack them tightly. Add the dry ingredients to a large, wide-mouthed mixing bowl, stir together to combine thoroughly, and then form a well in the center. I add the wet ingredients — dissolved yeast, water, eggs, oil, and so on — along with the starter, if

using, directly to the well. You may find it easier to whisk together the yeast mixture and other wet ingredients in a small bowl and then add them to the well.

MIXING   Using a sturdy wooden spoon, stir the dry ingredients into the wet ingredients by pulling the walls of the flour mixture into the well. Some doughs will come together quickly at this point; others will call for some hard work. When the dough is too stiff to stir, work it with your hands until it pulls away from the sides of the bowl and has a consistent texture. This will take less than a minute with some doughs and up to five minutes with others. Once the dough is ready, turn it out onto a lightly floured surface, easing it out of the bowl cleanly with the plastic dough scraper.

KNEADING BY HAND   Kneading involves basically three moves: folding the dough toward you, pushing it outward with the heels of your hands, and then rotating it a quarter of a turn. Repeat this simple pattern over and over until the dough reaches the consistency described in the individual recipes. If the dough is extremely soft or sticky — or the day is very humid — work in a little more flour, but add it only by *pinches.* Too much flour will result in a dry, disappointing loaf. If the dough begins to stick to the work surface, loosen it with a metal dough scaper and coat the work surface with a *light* dusting of flour.

EGG WATCH
❖

When adding eggs to a dough or batter, break them, one at a time, into a small bowl, to be sure that each egg is fresh before it is combined with the other ingredients.

Cold eggs do not achieve as much volume when beaten, which makes them less successful as leavening agents in cakes and cookies. If a recipe calls for separating the whites and yolks, do so while the eggs are still cold from the refrigerator; a cold yolk is less likely to break. Then let the whites and yolks come to room temperature before using.

SPONGES

❖

Some breads call for making a sponge, which is a loose, springy mixture of yeast, liquid, and dry ingredients that is allowed to stand for anywhere from an hour to overnight before the remaining ingredients are added to the dough. This lightly fermented mixture gives breads a more intense flavor. A sponge differs from a starter, or biga, in that the composition of a sponge and its timing is particular to a given recipe. A starter, in contrast, is a more universal ingredient; it is stored for long periods and can be added to countless bread doughs.

KNEADING BY MACHINE   Of course, the "equipment dependent" can bring out the mixer and dough hook or the food processor and blades and mix and partially knead doughs the modern way. (Check the manufacturer's instructions on your processor to see if it has a sufficiently strong motor for mixing bread doughs.) The loaves will still bake beautifully.

Doughs made in a mixer are generally assembled much the same way as they are by hand: dry ingredients are beaten into wet ingredients with a paddle attachment and then the dough hook is engaged for kneading. Doughs made in a food processor call for combining the dry ingredients in the work bowl and adding the wet ingredients through the feed tube, first mixing until a rough mass forms and then processing steadily to knead the dough. (Ingredients mixed in a processor should be cold, since the motor heats up the contents of the work bowl.) In both cases you must also knead the dough briefly by hand.

FIRST RISING   Once the dough is fully kneaded, shape it into a ball, place it in a large, lightly oiled bowl, and turn the ball so that the entire surface has a light coating of oil, to prevent it from sticking to the bowl. Cover the bowl with a cotton towel and leave the dough to rise at room temperature. The rising times given in the recipes reflect a temperature of about 70 degrees F. On warmer days, the bread will

rise more quickly; on cooler days, it will rise more slowly. (A slower rise produces a fuller-flavored loaf.)

SECOND RISING   When the dough has doubled in volume, deflate it by folding the edges in toward the center, then cover it and leave it to rise in the bowl again (or another vessel if specified in the recipe) until doubled. The second rising usually takes less time than the first. If at any point during these risings you are interrupted and must put off finishing the bread, slip the dough into the refrigerator or put it in a very cool place for a few hours — or even overnight, if necessary. Return it to room temperature before continuing.

SHAPING   Deflate the dough once again and then shape it according to the recipe directions. Do not overwork the dough at this point or you will weaken the gluten and it will tear instead of stretch in the heat of the oven, with the result that the bread will not rise properly. A metal dough scraper is ideal for cutting the dough into portions for forming into loaves or rolls. Leave the dough to rise, either on a work surface or a baker's peel, according to the recipe directions.

PREPARING THE OVEN   Place a baking stone on the lowest rack in an oven or line the oven floor with quarry tiles and preheat the oven for at least thirty minutes to ensure the baking surface is fully heated. Many recipes call for spray misting both the oven and the bread before the baking begins, to encourage nicely browned crusts. How much misting is appropriate depends upon the individual bread; the recipes will guide you.

USING A PEEL   Now comes the tricky part, moving the bread from the peel to the oven. Professional bakers and pizza chefs perform this movement effortlessly, holding the peel parallel to the stone and snapping the wrist with a precision that sends the shaped dough — a large domed loaf, a dozen square rolls, a spherical pizza crust — smoothly onto the stone. Do not space loaves or rolls too close together on the peel; their positions on the peel will be much the same as those on the stone, and to bake evenly, hot air must circulate around them freely. The only secret to success with the peel I know is practice.

BAKING   Because oven thermometers are not always accurate, begin checking the bread ten minutes before the baking time indicated in the recipe, and then every five minutes after that point. The venerable method for knowing when a bread is done is to knock your knuckles against the bottom and listen for a full, hollow sound. A dull thud means the bread needs a few more minutes. Breads baked on a sheet pan cook more quickly than those baked on a stone. After removing the loaves or rolls from the oven, cool them on racks so that air circulates around them.

STORING   Most breads and rolls are meant to be eaten the day they are baked. Round, crusty loaves tend to have longer lives. These loaves can be tucked into a paper bag or wrapped in a cotton towel and kept on a countertop for a day or two. Recipes indicate if the bread or rolls keep particularly well. The American custom of freezing baked breads is one that I cannot accept.

Baking Sweets

Many Italian sweets are rococo constructions of cream and custard, fondant sugar and chocolate glazes, fruits and nuts. I have chosen both home-style and elegant recipes, but none that requires complicated techniques to achieve a successful result. There are nut-laced cookie doughs that are mixed and formed simply; rich, flaky pastry shells that roll out with ease; and cake batters that whip up effortlessly.

I have included basic instructions in the recipe methods for such common dessert-making tasks as creaming butter and sugar, whipping egg whites, and lining tart tins with pastry. If you lack experience using a pastry bag, you may encounter some difficulty making perfectly shaped rosettes or topping a pie with meringue. Using these bags with confidence demands practice. You will also find a number of helpful hints included in introductions to recipes and in the margins.

LE RICETTE DEL FORNAIO

The Baker's Recipes

PANE TRADIZIONALE

Traditional Breads

These are our everyday breads, rustic loaves that have sustained Italians for centuries. They are the breads that rural people traditionally baked twice a week in charcoal-fired stone ovens that stood just outside their houses, and that city dwellers bought daily at a bakery in a nearby piazza. They are made from flour, water, salt, and yeast, and they are formed into dark rounds, long, slender batons, or flat rectangles.

I can remember as a five-year-old going out into the country with the family to visit my uncles, farmers whose land lay half a dozen miles from my hometown of Carpenedolo. There I watched my aunts as they worked huge mounds of dough into perfectly round loaves and then baked them in the outdoor *forno*. Five years later I bicycled along the same roads to deliver a variety of more refined bakery breads to dozens of farm families. During the snowy months, when the roads were treacherous and the deliveries stopped, the women would rely solely on their venerable stone ovens. This scene was replayed throughout rural Italy until the late 1960s, when bakeries became the source of the daily bread of rural and city people alike.

The bakeries in Carpenedolo — there were five in town when I was growing up, now there are seven or eight — have always made small breads — *panini* — rather than large loaves. The Italians are staunch culinary regionalists; today, with the exception of Il Fornaio and a few similar operations, it is the small local bakeries that concentrate on their area's specialties.

Of the ten breads in this chapter, four shine through as breads born from a truly grand tradition: *ciabatta*, *pagnotta*, *pane Altamura*, and *pane toscano*. All of them, however, are excellent accompaniments to any meal, from a simple repast of soup and *frittata* to a celebratory feast.

FILONE

PANE TOSCANO

PANE ETRUSCA

PANE ACIDO DI SEMOLA

PAGNOTTA

PANE TRADIZIONALE

SFILATINO

CIABATTA

PANE SICILIANO

PANE ALTAMURA

FOCACCIA ALLA GENOVESE

BIGA

Starter Dough

¾ teaspoon active dry
  yeast

½ cup warm water
  (105 degrees F)

3½ cups unbleached
  bread flour

1¼ cups cool water

A biga, or "starter," adds flavor and extra leavening power to bread dough. Before the advent of manufactured yeast, bakers relied solely on starters — "old dough" — for leavening, and at Il Fornaio we still make our sourdough breads with only a starter. In general, though, it is more practical and reliable to use a small amount of manufactured yeast in combination with a starter.

You may either halve this starter recipe or make a full recipe and freeze the leftover starter in one-quarter or one-half cup portions. Thaw at room temperature before using.

In a small bowl dissolve the yeast in the warm water. Set it aside until it is creamy, about 15 minutes.

Measure the flour into a large bowl. Using a sturdy wooden spoon, form a well in the center of the flour and add the yeast mixture and cool water to the well. Using the spoon stir together all the ingredients until sticky and difficult to stir but nevertheless thoroughly combined. Cover tightly and allow to ferment slowly in the refrigerator for 24 hours before using.

Store in the refrigerator for up to 2 weeks. To use, rinse a measuring cup in cool water, scoop out the amount of starter needed, and bring to room temperature.

BIGA ACIDA
Sourdough Starter Dough

◆

Sourdough starters can be tricky to make. Because chlorine or contaminants in tap water could spell failure, use only noncarbonated bottled water. To avoid unwanted yeast spores present in flour milled from pesticide-treated wheat, look for flour milled from organically grown wheat.

If after three days the starter produces no bubbles or has an unpleasant odor, it means that it has probably picked up one of the many wild yeasts present in the air. Throw it away before "feeding" it with more flour and water, and try again.

This starter will keep tightly covered in the refrigerator for up to two weeks without additional feeding, but it will be slow to revive. To encourage the starter, return it to room temperature for several days, adding flour and water every twenty-four hours. It will once again become active. Always feed it with equal parts flour and water and never in a greater amount than the already existing amount of the starter. As with the preceding starter recipe, you may either halve this starter recipe or freeze it in one-quarter or one-half cup portions. Thaw at room temperature before using.

2 cups organic whole-wheat flour

2 cups noncarbonated bottled water

Measure I cup of the flour into a bowl. Add I cup of the water and, using a sturdy wooden spoon, stir until thoroughly combined. Cover tightly and let stand at room temperature for 3 days, stirring it down once daily. The mixture will be pasty during this period; if it becomes too hard and dry to stir, stir in a little additional bottled water.

At the end of the third day, the starter will have a sour aroma and small bubbles will have formed on top. Now feed the starter by adding the remaining I cup flour and I cup water and stirring them in with the wooden spoon to incorporate thoroughly. Let stand at room temperature for 24 hours, at which point the starter is ready. To use, rinse a measuring cup in cool water and scoop out the amount of starter needed.

Italy is divided into two
types of bread eaters:
those who like
la crosta —
"the crust" — and those
who prefer
la mollica — "the
crumb." Proof of this
statement is always
present on trattoria
tables just after the
diners have left. Amidst
the dirty plates and
glasses are clumps of
la mollica, the white
insides of the bread,
evidence that crust lovers
ate there, or dark shards
of la crosta,
confirmation that la
mollica partisans have
just dined. I am a
dedicated crust person,
while my sister Teresa
favors the crumb. I tell
her that if she eats only
la mollica it is bad for
her digestion because it
sits like a lump in her
stomach. She tells me
that crust is hard on the
teeth. Italians are
stubborn about their
bread. Teresa and I will
never reconcile this
difference.

PAGNOTTA
Round Country Bread

◆

MAKES TWO 1 1/4-POUND LOAVES

Typical of central Italy — Tuscany, Umbria, Abruzzi — pagnotta *is a rustic peasant loaf with a hard, deep brown crust and a soft, white center. This is a bread that will keep well for two or three days. In fact, I prefer it on the second day; to my taste, the center is too soft the same day the loaf comes out of the oven.* Pagnotta *also can be found in northern Italy, although there the dough is more often made into* pagnottine *(directions follow), small round rolls that are sold in bakeries from Milan and Brescia to Verona and Venice.*

This same dough is used to make a number of other Il Fornaio breads and rolls, including the slipper-shaped ciabatta *and the square* panini del Fornaio. *It is a lean dough — no oil, butter, or eggs — so it is very forgiving when you leave it to rise. It can sit for only an hour or for as long as two hours and it will still bake just fine.*

Do not be disheartened if the loaves are not perfectly round. Shaping a beautiful pagnotta *takes practice. And even though your initial attempts at forming symmetrical loaves may fail, your first* pagnotte *will still taste wonderful.*

In a small bowl dissolve the yeast in the warm water. Set it aside until it is creamy, about 15 minutes.

Measure the flour into a large bowl. Using a sturdy wooden spoon, stir the salt into the flour. Form a well in the center of the flour mixture and add the yeast mixture, the cool water, and the *biga* to the well. Using the spoon stir together all the ingredients until the dough is too resistant to be stirred. They will come together fairly easily.

Now begin kneading the dough in the bowl, keeping one hand clean in order to hold and turn the bowl and using the other hand to work the dough. Vigorously fold the dough from the sides of the bowl toward the center, rotating the bowl as you work. Pick up the dough and slap it back into the bowl several times and keep kneading vigorously. The dough will be slightly sticky, but continue working it until it comes away cleanly from the sides of the bowl. This should take about 5 minutes.

At this point turn the dough out onto a lightly floured work surface. Clean off any dough stuck to your hands and then knead the dough until it is stretchy, smooth and fairly soft. This will take 15 to 20 minutes of kneading, including some 1- to 2-minute rest periods along the way for the dough to relax slightly — and for you to relax, too. Shape the dough into a ball.

Rub a large bowl with olive oil and place the dough in the bowl. Turn the ball so that the surface is coated with oil. Cover the bowl with a towel and let the dough rise at room temperature until doubled, about 1½ hours.

Punch down the dough by folding the edges into the center and turning it over so the top is once again smooth. Re-cover the bowl and let the dough rise a second time until doubled, about 1 hour.

Turn the dough out onto a lightly floured work surface. Divide the dough into 2 equal portions. Working with 1 portion at a time and trying not to overhandle the dough, fold the edges in toward the center. Work in a circular motion, folding the entire rim of the dough in toward the center several times to form a round ball with a smooth side.

Spread a fairly thick layer of flour on a work surface. Place the ball of dough, rough side down, on the flour. Shape the remaining portion into a second loaf and place it on the surface in the same manner. Cover the loaves with a towel and let rise at room temperature for 40 to 55 minutes. Meanwhile, place a baking stone in an oven and preheat to 425 degrees F.

About 40 minutes after the loaves have been rising, test one by lightly pushing your index finger into it and then removing your finger. If the dough springs back gently, it is ready to bake. If the indentation does not move, your dough has risen too much and will not "jump" (rise) in the oven. If the latter is the case, reform the loaves in the same manner and let rise again for 40 to 55 minutes.

Dust a baker's peel with cornmeal. Gently slip your hand under each loaf and turn it over onto the peel, so the rough side now faces up. Mist the preheated oven with a spray bottle. With a rhythmic snap of the wrist, slide the loaves onto

1½ teaspoons active dry yeast

½ cup warm water (105 degrees F)

7 cups unbleached bread flour

1 tablespoon salt

2¾ cups cool water

¾ cup Biga (page 32)

Additional flour for work surface

Olive oil for bowl

Medium-grind yellow cornmeal for baker's peel

the baking stone. Mist the oven again and bake the breads for 5 minutes. Mist one more time, reduce the oven temperature to 400 degrees F, and bake until the loaves have a hollow ring when tapped on the bottom, 40 to 50 minutes. When the loaves are done, their tops should have an attractive pattern of white flour, their sides should be deep golden brown, and their bottoms should be quite dark. Remove to wire racks to cool completely.

PAGNOTTINE *Round Country Rolls* Prepare the dough as directed for *pagnotta* to the point where it is formed into loaves. Divide the dough into twenty-four 2-ounce portions. Form each portion into a ball by rolling each small piece of dough between your cupped hand and a flour-dusted work surface. As each ball is formed, shape it into a round roll by folding the edges into the center in the same manner as for the loaves.

Following the directions for the loaves, let the rolls rise, load them onto the cornmeal-dusted baker's peel, and slide them onto a baking stone in an oven preheated to 425 degrees F. Remember to mist the oven before and just after putting the rolls into it. Bake for 5 minutes, mist again, and reduce the oven temperature to 400 degrees F. Bake until the rolls have a hollow ring when tapped on the bottom, 20 to 30 minutes. When the rolls are done, they will be a rich dark color and have the same inviting flour pattern on top as the loaves do. Cool on wire racks. Makes twenty-four 2-ounce rolls.

◆　　◆　　◆

CIABATTA
Slipper-Shaped Bread

MAKES TWO 1 1/4-POUND LOAVES

The region between Lake Como and Milan, called the Brianza, is noted for furniture making (and as the setting of I promessi sposi, *or "The betrothed," Italy's most famous novel). It is also home to the* ciabatta, *or "slipper." The dough is the same as for* pagnotta; *the shape, loosely reminiscent of a slipper, makes it distinctive.* Ciabatta *is a crusty, porous loaf with big* occhi *("eyes") inside, made from an elastic dough that must be "pulled" into its unique form. In* caffè *in Italy you will find* ciabattine — *half-size* ciabatte — *split and filled with prosciutto or salami.*

1 recipe Pagnotta dough (page 34)

Olive oil for dish

Unbleached bread flour for work surface

Medium-grind yellow cornmeal for baker's peel

Prepare the dough for *pagnotta* through the first rising. Rub a baking dish about 8 inches square (or a rectangular dish of roughly the same size) with a liberal amount of olive oil. Turn the risen dough out into it. Press the dough evenly into the dish, making certain that it fits the corners snugly; it should reach no more than halfway up the sides. Cover and let rise at room temperature until doubled, about 1½ hours.

Gently invert the risen dough out onto a well-floured work surface. Divide the dough into 2 rectangles. Working with 1 rectangle at a time, gently press out most of the air. Then pull the long cut side farthest from you toward you halfway over the dough so that it rests on top in the middle of the rectangle.

Gently transfer the loaves to a well-floured surface and cover. Let rise for 45 minutes. Meanwhile, place a baking stone in an oven and preheat to 425 degrees F.

Sprinkle some flour onto the top of each loaf and gently turn each loaf over. Do this quickly and confidently and you will avoid leaving finger marks. Now the loaves are upright and each is topped with a flour pattern that will bake into the loaf later. Each loaf should be about 15 inches long, 3½ inches wide, and ¾ inch thick. Cover and let rise a final 15 minutes.

Mist the preheated oven with a spray bottle and quickly shut the oven door. Dust a baker's peel with cornmeal. Gently transfer the loaves to the peel and mist them. With a rhythmic snap of the wrist, slide the loaves onto the baking stone. Mist the oven again and bake the loaves until they are dark brown on the bottom, golden brown on the top and sides, and have a hollow ring when tapped on the bottom, about 1 hour. Remove to wire racks to cool completely.

*Italians value salt highly
— so highly, in fact, that
until recently the
government exercised a
monopoly on its sale.
My mother still recalls
the war years, when salt
was precious and all she
could find was black
mineral salt from the
mountains.*

*The finest Italian salt
comes straight from the
sea, is absolutely pure,
and tastes a hundred
times better than
American salt. For years
I tried to import this
superior salt for use in
the Il Fornaio
restaurants, but the
government's control kept
me from doing so.
Finally, in 1991,
following the repeal of
the monopoly, I was able
to bring in salt from
Sicily's Golfo di Carini,
near Palermo. I consider
Carini salt the best in
all of Italy. Every Il
Fornaio restaurant
saltshaker now holds this
extraordinary product.*

PANE TOSCANO
Saltless Bread from Tuscany

◆

MAKES TWO 1 1/4-POUND LOAVES OR FOUR 10-OUNCE LOAVES

If you were to suggest a saltless loaf to any Italian other than a Tuscan, the idea would immediately be dismissed as bread heresy. So why are the Tuscans different? Some culinary pundits theorize that the relative scarcity and high cost of salt in banking-minded Florence prompted enterprising bakers to develop a salt-free pane. I, however, side with those who believe the Tuscans created this exceptional bread because they preferred it. They knew that a salted loaf would detract from the flavor of their prized prosciutto toscano, which is customarily saltier than the prosciutto produced in other parts of Italy. Eating a chunk of regular bread topped with a slice of Florentine prosciutto would be like eating it with anchovies.

The Tuscans were also wary of masking the flavor of yet another famous local product, the fruity green olive oil of Lucca. They pair the fragrant oil with bread in a traditional preparation called la fettunta, literally "oily slice" (la fetta, "slice," and unta, from ungere, "to put oil on"). It is the simplest of gastronomic pleasures: a crusty round of pane toscano smeared with some deep green olive oil and gently warmed.

This bread dough is similar to that for pagnotta (page 34), except for the absence of salt and a smaller amount of water. Salt slows fermentation, so this dough rises quite quickly, and the reduced water produces a less sticky dough that is easier to knead.

In a small bowl dissolve the yeast in the warm water. Set it aside until it is creamy, about 15 minutes.

Measure the flour into a large bowl. Using a sturdy wooden spoon, form a well in the center of the flour and add the yeast mixture, the cool water, and the *biga* to the well. Using the spoon stir together all the ingredients until the dough is too resistant to be stirred. They will come together fairly easily.

Now begin kneading the dough in the bowl, keeping one hand clean in order to hold and turn the bowl and using the other hand to work the dough. Vigorously fold the dough from the sides of the bowl toward the center, rotating the bowl as you work. Pick up the dough and slap it back into the bowl several times and keep kneading vigorously until the dough comes away cleanly from the sides of the bowl. This should take about 5 minutes.

At this point turn the dough out onto a lightly floured work surface and clean off any dough stuck to your hands. Knead the dough until it is stretchy, smooth, and fairly soft, about 20 minutes, including some 1- to 2-minute rest periods along the way. Shape the dough into a ball.

Rub a large bowl with olive oil and place the dough in the bowl. Turn the ball so that the surface is coated with oil. Cover the bowl with a towel and let the dough rise at room temperature until doubled, about 1 hour.

Rub a baking dish about 6 inches square (or a rectangular dish of roughly the same size) with a liberal amount of olive oil. Turn the risen dough out into it. With your fingertips press the dough evenly into the dish, making certain that it fits snugly into the corners; it should reach no more than halfway up the sides of the dish. Cover with a towel and let rise at room temperature until doubled, about 50 minutes. Meanwhile, place a baking stone in an oven and preheat to 425 degrees F.

Gently invert the risen dough out onto a well-floured work surface. Divide the dough into 2 large rectangles or 4 small rectangles. Dust a baker's peel with cornmeal. Again working very gently so as not to deflate the dough, turn the rectangles upright and place them on the peel.

Mist the preheated oven with a spray bottle. With a rhythmic snap of the wrist, slide the loaves onto the baking stone. Mist the oven again and bake the breads for 5 minutes. Mist one more time and then bake until the crusts are a deep golden brown and the loaves have a hollow ring when tapped on the bottom, 45 to 50 minutes for the small loaves and 55 minutes for the large loaves. Remove to wire racks to cool completely.

2 teaspoons active dry yeast

½ cup warm water (105 degrees F)

5½ cups unbleached bread flour

2¼ cups cool water

½ cup Biga (page 32)

Additional flour for work surface

Olive oil for bowl and dish

Medium-grind yellow cornmeal for baker's peel

FOCACCIA ALLA GENOVESE
Olive Oil Flat Bread from Genoa

◆

MAKES ONE 8-INCH SQUARE; 18 OUNCES

½ teaspoon active dry yeast

½ cup warm water (105 degrees F)

2½ cups unbleached bread flour

½ teaspoon salt

½ cup cool water

1 tablespoon extra-virgin olive oil

¼ cup Biga (page 32)

Additional flour for work surface

Additional olive oil for bowl and bread

Medium-grind yellow cornmeal for baker's peel

For years, San Francisco, a favorite destination for Ligurian immigrants at the turn of the century, was the only place in America that boasted genuine focaccia, the famed Genoese flat bread that is delicious served with salads, soups, or even alone as a snack.

In a small bowl dissolve the yeast in the warm water. Set it aside until it is creamy, about 15 minutes.

Measure the flour into a large mixing bowl. Using a sturdy wooden spoon, stir the salt into the flour. Form a well in the center of the flour mixture and add the yeast mixture, the cool water, the olive oil, and the *biga* to the well. Using the spoon stir together all the ingredients until the dough is too resistant to be stirred.

Knead the dough briefly in the bowl and then turn it out onto a lightly floured work surface and clean off any dough stuck to your hands. Knead vigorously until it is smooth and elastic, about 20 minutes, including some 1- to 2-minute rest periods along the way. The dough will be somewhat sticky until it is fully kneaded. Shape the dough into a ball.

Rub a large bowl with olive oil and place the dough in the bowl. Turn the ball so that the surface is coated with oil. Cover the bowl with a towel and let the dough rise at room temperature until doubled, about 1½ hours.

Punch down the dough by folding the edges into the center and turning it over so the top is once again smooth. Re-cover the bowl and let the dough rise a second time until doubled, about 45 minutes.

Turn the dough out onto a lightly floured work surface. Using the palms of your hands, gently press it out into an 8-inch square about ¾ inch thick. Flour a second surface, slip both hands under the square, and move it to the new surface. Cover with a towel and let rise until doubled, about 50 minutes. Meanwhile, place a baking stone in an oven and preheat to 425 degrees F.

Mist the preheated oven with a spray bottle and quickly shut the door. Dust a baker's peel with cornmeal. Gently transfer the dough square to the baker's peel. Using a soft-bristled brush, paint the surface of the square with olive oil. Using your fingertips, press "dimples" all over the surface of the dough; they should be about three quarters the depth of the thickness of the square. Mist the square. With a rhythmic snap of the wrist, slide the square onto the baking stone. Mist the oven again and bake for 5 minutes. Mist one more time and bake the focaccia until it is golden brown, about 30 minutes. Remove from the oven to a wire rack, brush with olive oil, and cool completely.

SFILATINO
Italian Baguette

◆

MAKES THREE 7-OUNCE LOAVES

The true baguette, of course, was born in France, just prior to World War I, when the citizenry demanded an alternative to the standard round and rectangular loaves of the day. The French wanted more crust and less mie, which is what they call a bread's interior in France (the mollica, in Italian). The baguette was the bakers' solution. The sfilatino came about for the same reason — consumer demand. Italians developed a taste for the French baguette, and Italian bakers, who always love a challenge, set out to better it.

In a small bowl dissolve the yeast in the warm water. Set it aside until it is creamy, about 15 minutes.

Measure the flour into a large bowl. Using a sturdy wooden spoon, stir the salt into the flour. Form a well in the center of the flour mixture and add the yeast mixture, the cool water, and the *biga* to the well. Using the spoon stir together all the ingredients until the dough is too resistant to be stirred. This dough has a relatively low water content, so it will come together fairly easily.

Knead the dough briefly in the bowl, and then turn it out onto a lightly floured work surface and clean off any dough stuck to your hands. Knead the dough until it is smooth, silky, and noticeably elastic, about 20 minutes, including several 1- to 2-minute rest periods along the way. Shape the dough into a ball.

Rub a large bowl with olive oil and place the dough in the bowl. Turn the ball so that the surface is coated with oil. Cover the bowl with a towel and let the dough rise at room temperature until doubled, about 1½ hours.

PANE
DI FICHI

◆

Although the oldest fig tree in the world reputedly stands in Palermo's Garibaldi garden and most of Italy's figs are grown in the sunny south, pane di fichi is a Milanese specialty. Undoubtedly the fruit for these loaves is plucked from the fig groves that stand not far from Lake Como. The bread is similar to the long, slender sfilatino, with a single row of plump, round figs concealed in its center. When the bread is cut, each slice produces a beautiful cross section of the fruit. Pane di fichi is costly in Italy, and people in the north, with their booming economy, are better able to afford it than their measurably poorer cousins in the Mezzogiorno.

Punch down the dough by folding the edges into the center and turning it over so the top is once again smooth. Press most but not all of the air out of the dough. Re-cover the bowl and let the dough rise at room temperature a second time until doubled, about 1 hour.

Turn the dough out onto a lightly floured work surface. Divide the dough into 3 equal portions. Working with 1 portion at a time and using your fingertips, gently press out most of the air as you form the dough into a rectangle measuring 4 by 3 inches. Fold about 1 inch of the long rectangle edge farthest from you toward you. Then continue to roll up the rectangle toward you, in the same manner as you would wrap silverware in a cloth napkin. Try to introduce some tension into the roll so that it is fairly tight. When you reach the edge nearest you, using the heel of your hand, press the edge of the roll to the bottom edge of the rectangle to form a seam. The roll should be about 6 inches long. Repeat with the remaining dough portions.

Turn each roll so that it rests seam side down on a well-floured work surface. Taper the ends of the rolls by simultaneously rolling and pressing them against the work surface with the palms of your hands. Let rise, uncovered, at room temperature, for 20 minutes. The dough will relax during this period and become even more elastic. Meanwhile, place a baking stone in an oven and preheat to 425 degrees F.

Grasp the ends of one roll and lift it from the work surface. Stretch the roll until it is roughly two and a half times its original length, or about 15 inches long. Return it to the work surface. Repeat with the remaining dough rolls and then let the loaves rest for 10 to 15 minutes longer.

Mist the preheated oven with a spray bottle and quickly shut the oven door. Dust a baker's peel with cornmeal. Gently transfer the loaves to the baker's peel. Using a sharp serrated knife, make 5 diagonal slashes about ½ inch deep on the top of each loaf. Mist the loaves generously. With a rhythmic snap of the wrist, slide the loaves onto the baking stone. Mist the oven again and bake the breads for 5 minutes. Mist one more time and bake the loaves until they have golden brown, crisp crusts and produce a hollow ring when tapped on the bottom, 25 to 35 minutes. Remove to wire racks to cool completely.

1 teaspoon active dry yeast

½ cup warm water (105 degrees F)

3 cups unbleached bread flour

1 rounded teaspoon salt

½ cup plus 2 tablespoons cool water

½ cup Biga (page 32)

Additional flour for work surface

Olive oil for bowl

Medium-grind yellow cornmeal for baker's peel

◆ ◆ ◆

PANE ETRUSCA
Etruscan Bread

MAKES TWO 1-POUND LOAVES

Three cultures — the Etruscan, Greek, and Saracen — formed the foundation for contemporary Italian cuisine. In preparation for the opening of the Etrusca restaurant in San Francisco in 1990, I pored over dozens of volumes to gather as much knowledge as possible about the Etruscan table, to create a menu that drew upon the legacy of this mysterious civilization.

What information does exist on the Etruscans comes down to us from the conquering Romans, who recorded that the vanquished ate, among other things, round, flat breads, depictions of which can still be seen on the walls of Etruscan ruins. Our complexly flavored bread — mildly tangy from the buttermilk — was inspired by those early drawings.

The disks need not be perfectly round. A slightly rustic appearance is desirable, for the idea is to simulate a flat bread as it may have appeared during Etruscan times, before leavening methods were perfected.

To make the sponge, in a small bowl dissolve the yeast in the warm water. Set it aside until it is creamy, about 15 minutes.

Measure the bread flour into a large mixing bowl. Using a sturdy wooden spoon, form a well in the center of the flour and add the yeast mixture and the cool water to the well. Using the spoon stir together all of the ingredients until the dough is too resistant to be stirred.

Now begin kneading the dough in the bowl, keeping one hand clean in order to hold and turn the bowl and using the other hand to work the dough. Vigorously fold the dough from the sides of the bowl toward the center, rotating the bowl as you work. Pick up the dough and slap it back into the bowl several times and keep

STAYING POWER
❖

Round loaves, such as pane Etrusca *and* pagnotta, *last longer than slender breads — sometimes up to three days when wrapped in a light towel and left on the kitchen counter. The greater expanse of crust on a round loaf keeps the soft center from drying out.*

When I was a teenager I visited a family in the Etruscan hills north of Rome. They were farmers and lived without electricity or running water. For dinner we ate the farm's own bounty: chicken roasted on a spit, goat cheese, and chunks of bread cut from large, round, crusty loaves. The family made bread just once a week and it stayed fresh until the next batch was baked.

kneading vigorously until the dough comes away cleanly from the sides of the bowl. This should take about 5 minutes.

At this point turn the dough out onto a lightly floured work surface and clean off any dough stuck to your hands. Knead the dough until it is smooth and velvety, 20 to 25 minutes, including some 1- to 2-minute rest periods along the way. Shape the dough into a ball.

Rub a large bowl with olive oil and place the dough in the bowl. Turn the ball so that the surface is coated with oil. Cover the bowl with a towel and let the dough rise at room temperature until slightly more than doubled, about 1½ hours.

Now add the bran, cornmeal, whole-wheat flour, olive oil, buttermilk, salt, and molasses to the risen sponge. Using your hands mix in the ingredients and knead the dough as described above, working very gently or the coarse bran and cornmeal will "tear" the gluten and the bread will not rise. Do not panic when the dough begins to break up; it will come together again after about 5 minutes of kneading. Shape the dough into a ball.

Rub a second large bowl with olive oil and place the dough in the bowl. Again turn the ball to coat the surface with oil, cover, and let rise until doubled, about 1 hour.

Turn the dough out onto a lightly floured work surface. Divide the dough into 2 equal portions. Working with 1 portion at a time and trying not to overhandle the dough, fold the edges in toward the center. Work in a circular motion, folding the entire rim of the dough in toward the center several times to form a round ball with a smooth side.

Spread a fairly thick layer of flour on a work surface. Place the ball of dough, rough side down, on the flour. Shape the remaining portion into a second loaf and place it on the surface in the same manner. Cover the loaves with a towel and let rise at room temperature until almost doubled, about 45 minutes. Meanwhile, place a baking stone in an oven and preheat to 400 degrees F.

With your fingertips gently press out each loaf, leaving deep "dimples" in the surface of the dough and forming a disk about 6 inches in diameter and ¾ inch thick. Do not flatten them any more than that. Let the loaves rest for 10 to 15 minutes.

Mist the preheated oven with a spray bottle and quickly shut the oven door. Dust a baker's peel with cornmeal. Gently transfer the loaves to the peel, sprinkle some cornmeal on top of the loaves, and lightly mist them. With a rhythmic snap of the wrist, slide the loaves onto the baking stone. Bake the loaves until they are evenly tan and have a hollow ring when tapped on the bottom, 30 to 35 minutes. Remove to wire racks to cool completely.

For the sponge:

1½ teaspoons active dry yeast

½ cup warm water (105 degrees F)

3½ cups unbleached bread flour

1 cup cool water

Additional flour for work surface

Olive oil for bowl

¼ cup unprocessed wheat bran

2 tablespoons medium-grind yellow cornmeal

5 tablespoons whole-wheat flour

¼ cup extra-virgin olive oil

3 tablespoons buttermilk

1 tablespoon salt

2 teaspoons molasses

Additional olive oil for bowl

Additional cornmeal for baker's peel and loaves

PANE ALTAMURA

Bread from Altamura

MAKES ONE 1-POUND LOAF

Altamura lies twenty-five miles inland from the port of Bari in Apulia, near the heel of the Italian boot. It is the principal town of the Murge, an expanse of plains and gentle hills, and a lovely cathedral begun early in the thirteenth century stands majestically in its main piazza. The structure has an unusual history. It sustained great damage in an earthquake in the early fourteenth century. During the Renaissance it was rebuilt; in that process a pair of towers was added and the portal and exquisite rose window were disassembled and then reconstructed where the apse had previously stood. In other words, what was once the back of the cathedral became the front, making it unique amongst the wealth of sacred buildings in Italy. The area beyond Altamura is carpeted in fields of wheat and other cereals, the source of the flours that go into the remarkable local breads.

Here is a heavy country bread that is typical of the loaves found in the town and the surrounding countryside. The dough, which is made from bread flour and semolina, bakes up into a round, crusty loaf with a pale ivory interior and a distinctive, quite wonderful flavor that complements almost any menu.

◆ ◆ ◆

The importance of bread in the Italian diet is reflected in many religious rituals, and arguably no region in Italy practices more of these rituals than Sicily. Mary Taylor Simetti, in her incomparable Pomp and Sustenance, *a highly memorable look at twenty-five centuries of Sicilian food, reports that the island women traditionally recited specific prayers as they kneaded and shaped the loaves. Later, the man of the house would always bless each loaf with the sign of the cross before cutting it. In central Sicily, wheat sheaves are a customary offering to the Virgin Mary, and the festival of San Giuseppe, which falls on March 19, is always celebrated with elaborate altar offerings sculpted from bread dough and a meal that has freshly baked* pane *as its centerpiece.*

In a small bowl dissolve the yeast in the warm water. Set it aside until it is creamy, about 15 minutes.

Measure the flours into a large bowl. Using a sturdy wooden spoon, stir the salt into the flours. Form a well in the center of the flour mixture and add the yeast mixture, the cool water, the olive oil, and the *biga* to the well. Using the spoon stir together all the ingredients until the dough is too resistant to be stirred.

Knead the dough briefly in the bowl and then turn it out onto a lightly floured work surface and clean off any dough stuck to your hands. Begin kneading the dough. It will be a bit sticky because of its relatively high water content, but do not despair. It will become smooth, silky, and elastic after about 20 minutes of kneading, including some 1- to 2-minute rest periods along the way. Shape the dough into a ball.

Rub a large bowl with olive oil and place the dough in the bowl. Turn the ball so that the surface is coated with oil. Cover the bowl with a towel and let the dough rise at room temperature until doubled, about 1 hour.

Punch down the dough by folding the edges into the center and turning it over so the top is once again smooth. Press most but not all of the air out of the dough. Re-cover the bowl and let the dough rise at room temperature a second time until doubled, about 45 minutes.

Turn the dough out onto a lightly floured work surface. Trying not to overwork the dough, fold the edges in toward the center. Work in a circular motion, folding the entire rim of the dough in toward the center several times to form a round ball with a smooth side.

Spread a fairly thick layer of flour on a work surface. Place the ball of dough, rough side down, on the flour. Cover the loaf with a towel and let rise at room temperature until doubled, 50 to 60 minutes. The dough is ready when it springs back gently upon being lightly pressed with your index finger. Meanwhile, place a baking stone in an oven and preheat to 425 degrees F.

Mist the preheated oven with a spray bottle and quickly shut the oven door. Dust a baker's peel with cornmeal. Gently transfer the loaf to the baker's peel. Using a sharp serrated knife, make 5 slashes about ½ inch deep and 2½ inches long on the top of the loaf. Mist the loaf generously. With a rhythmic snap of the wrist, slide the loaf onto the baking stone. Mist the oven again and bake the bread for 5 minutes. Mist one more time and bake the loaf until it is golden brown on top, dark brown on the bottom, and has a hollow ring when tapped on the bottom, 40 to 50 minutes. Remove to a wire rack to cool completely.

1 teaspoon active dry yeast

½ cup warm water (105 degrees F)

1½ cups unbleached bread flour

1 cup plus 1 tablespoon semolina flour

1¼ teaspoons salt

½ cup cool water

1 tablespoon extra-virgin olive oil

¼ cup Biga (page 32)

Additional flour for work surface

Additional olive oil for bowl

Medium-grind yellow cornmeal for baker's peel

FILONE
Cigar-Shaped Bread

1 recipe Pagnotta dough (page 34)

Olive oil for dish

Unbleached bread flour for work surface

Medium-grind yellow cornmeal for baker's peel

This white bread, with a crisp, thin crust and soft interior, originated in Milan and is similar to a French loaf. It is a perfect dinner bread with everything from a Caesar salad to grilled trout or roast chicken. At the Il Fornaio restaurants we also use it for bruschetta *(page 116)*, but it is the ideal base for French toast, too.

Prepare the dough for *pagnotta* through the first rising.

Rub a baking dish about 6 inches square (or a rectangular dish of roughly the same size) with a liberal amount of olive oil. Turn the risen dough out into it. With your fingertips press the dough evenly into the dish, making certain that it fits snugly into the corners; it should reach no more than halfway up the sides of the dish. Cover with a towel and let rise at room temperature until doubled, about 1½ hours.

Gently invert the risen dough out onto a well-floured work surface. Divide the dough into 2 equal portions. Working with 1 portion at a time and using your fingertips, gently press out most of the air as you form the dough into a 6- or 7-inch square. Fold about 1 inch of the square edge farthest from you toward you. Then continue to roll up the square toward you, in the same manner as you would wrap silverware in a cloth napkin. Try to introduce some tension into the roll so that it is fairly tight. When you reach the edge nearest you, using the heel of your hand, press the edge of the roll to the bottom edge of the square to form a seam. Repeat with the remaining dough portion.

Turn each loaf so that it rests seam side down on a well-floured work surface. Taper the ends of the loaves by simultaneously rolling and pressing them against the work surface with the palms of your hands. Cover with a towel and let rise at room temperature until doubled, about 1 hour. Meanwhile, place a baking stone in an oven and preheat to 425 degrees F.

Mist the preheated oven with a spray bottle and quickly shut the oven door. Dust a baker's peel with cornmeal. Gently transfer the loaves to the peel and mist them generously. With a rhythmic snap of the wrist, slide the loaves onto the baking stone. Bake the breads for 5 minutes and then mist the oven again. Continue baking the loaves until they are golden brown and have a hollow ring when tapped on the bottom, 55 to 60 minutes. Remove to wire racks to cool completely.

PANE SICILIANO
Bread from Sicily

The Sicilians, who have always regarded bread with unwavering respect, shape it in myriad ways. Some loaves are round, some long, some braided, some with a hole in the center; some look like a flower, others like an opened fan. For a midday snack Sicilians like to eat their bread with a companatico, *an "accompaniment" of green or black olives or an anchovy fillet or two. But Il Fornaio's Sicilian loaf itself makes an excellent* companatico, *particularly to soups and salads.*

1 recipe Pane Altamura *dough* (page 46)

Unbleached bread flour for work surface

½ cup sesame seeds

Medium-grind yellow cornmeal for baker's peel

Prepare the dough for *pane Altamura* through the second rising.

Turn the dough out onto a well-floured work surface. Fold the edges in toward the center. Work in a circular motion, folding the entire rim of the dough in toward the center twice to form a loose round ball with a smooth side.

Lightly press the ball into a disk about 6 inches in diameter and 1 inch thick. Lift up the far edge of the disk and fold it toward you, to rest on top of the disk, so that only one third of the disk remains uncovered. Lift the folded edge and roll it up toward you until the dough takes on a football shape. When you reach the edge nearest you, using the heel of your hand, press the edge of the roll to the bottom edge of the disk to form a seam.

Turn the loaf so that it rests seam side down on the work surface. Taper the ends of the loaf by simultaneously rolling and pressing them against the work surface with the palms of your hands. Using a spray bottle lightly mist the loaf. Spread the sesame seeds in a thin layer on the work sur-face and roll the loaf in the seeds to coat evenly. Lift the loaf and, pulling it into a soft crescent shape, place it seam side down on a lightly floured work surface. Using a sharp serrated knife cut "toes" along the convex side of the cres-cent, making the cuts ¾ inch deep and ¾ inch apart. Spread the toes apart slightly. Cover with a towel and let rise at room temperature until dou-bled, 45 to 55 minutes. The dough is ready when it springs back gently upon being lightly pressed with your index finger. Meanwhile, place a baking stone in an oven and preheat to 425 degrees F.

Mist the oven and quickly shut the oven door. Dust a baker's peel with cornmeal. Gently transfer the loaf to the peel and mist it gener-ously. With a rhythmic snap of the wrist, slide the loaf onto the baking stone. Mist the oven again and bake the bread for 5 minutes. Mist one more time and bake the loaf until it is golden brown and has a hollow ring when tapped on the bottom, about 45 minutes. Remove to a wire rack to cool completely.

PANE ACIDO DI SEMOLA

Sourdough Whole-Wheat Bread

MAKES ONE 18-OUNCE LOAF

This recipe is a reminder that not all Italian culinary creations come from Italy. San Francisco's Italian Americans have long blended their city's celebrated sourdough with the baking traditions of the old country.

Before making this bread, a sponge must be made and left to sit overnight. It gives the loaf a fine texture and a full, deep flavor. At Il Fornaio we have found that we can further enhance the flavor of the bakery's sourdough loaves with an addition that every Italian would applaud. We gather grape must from local wine makers and use it to develop natural yeasts for boosting the sourdough.

For extra crunch and flavor, gently roll the shaped loaf in sesame seeds or poppy seeds before baking.

◆　◆　◆

To make the sponge, in a mixing bowl place the *biga acida*, water, and flours. Using a sturdy wooden spoon, stir together all the ingredients until well mixed, 2 to 3 minutes. Cover the bowl with a towel and set aside at room temperature overnight.

The next day measure the flour into a large mixing bowl. Using the wooden spoon, stir the salt into the flour. Form a well in the center of the flour mixture and add the sponge (there should be about 1½ cups) and the water. Using the spoon stir together all the ingredients until the dough is too resistant to be stirred.

Knead the dough briefly in the bowl and then turn it out onto a lightly floured work surface and clean off any dough stuck to your hands. Knead vigorously until it is smooth and elastic, about 20 minutes with 1- to 2-minute rest periods along the way. Shape the dough into a ball.

Rub a large bowl with olive oil and place the dough in the bowl. Turn the ball so that the surface is coated with oil. Cover the bowl with a towel and let the dough rise at room temperature until doubled, about 3 hours.

Punch down the dough by folding the edges into the center and turning it over so the top is once again smooth. Press most but not all of the air out of the dough. Re-cover the bowl and let the dough rise at room temperature a second time until doubled, about 1½ hours.

Turn the dough out onto a lightly floured work surface. Trying not to overwork the dough, fold the edges in toward the center. Work in a circular motion, folding the entire rim of the dough in toward the center several times to form a round ball with a smooth side.

Spread a fairly thick layer of flour on a work surface. Place the ball of dough, rough side down, on the flour. Cover with a towel and let rise at room temperature for 1 hour. The dough is ready when it springs back gently upon being lightly pressed with your index finger. Meanwhile, place a baking stone in an oven and preheat to 400 degrees F.

Mist the preheated oven with a spray bottle and quickly shut the oven door. Dust a baker's peel with cornmeal. Gently transfer the loaf to the baker's peel. Using a sharp serrated knife, make 5 slashes about ½ inch deep and 2½ inches long on the top of the loaf. Mist the loaf generously. With a rhythmic snap of the wrist, slide the loaf onto the baking stone. Mist the oven again and bake the bread for 5 minutes. Mist one more time and bake the loaf until it is brown and blistered on top, dark brown on the bottom, and has a hollow ring when tapped on the bottom, 40 to 50 minutes. Remove to wire rack to cool completely.

For the sponge:

¼ cup Biga Acida (page 33)

6 tablespoons water

¼ cup unbleached all-purpose flour

6 tablespoons whole-wheat flour

1¾ cups unbleached all-purpose flour

½ teaspoon salt

Scant ½ cup water

Additional flour for work surface

Olive oil for bowl

Medium-grind yellow cornmeal for baker's peel

Pane Speciale

Special Breads

ational cuisines are constantly evolving, and Italian cuisine is no exception. Although many bakers in small-town Italy continue to make only traditional loaves, others have introduced new tastes into this Italian staple. The result has been the appearance of "special breads" — flavored with rosemary, dotted with nuts, packed with healthful grains — in selected *panetterie* throughout the boot.

Not all of the breads in this chapter fall into the category of *la nuova cucina*. Some are "special" because, for Italians, they are more than just everyday breads. One of those exceptional breads is *pane all'uva*. It is a loaf that always brings back memories of my father.

He was a furniture maker and labored alongside his own father in our family shop, which made handcrafted violins and other musical instruments as well. Sometimes I would join my father on his walk to Brescia to buy wood for his work. On the way home I was always tired, and we would stop at a small *panificio* where he bought me freshly baked raisin bread. *Pane all'uva* was considered a luxury at the time (and still is because of the high cost of raisins in Italy) and it was my reward for walking such a long distance.

Some of these recipes are traditional celebratory loaves, such as the Lombardian Christmas *panettone* and the dove-shaped *colomba pasquale*. Others reflect the interest in breads that use ingredients only recently introduced into the kitchens of Italian bakers. Still others are Il Fornaio favorites — breads that are requested time and again by our customers.

COLOMBA PASQUALE

PANE DI NOVE CEREALI

PANE ALLE NOCI

CHALLAH

Pane Speciale

Pane alle Olive

Pane alle Patate

Pane all'Uva

Panmarino

Panettone

*The olive tree is believed
to have been first
cultivated in present-day
Syria and Palestine some
four thousand years
ago. The ancient
Romans planted trees
about five centuries later,
and the locals were quick
to make these fruits —
along with bread —
dietary staples. Today
olive groves are tended in
many parts of Italy, and
the oil pressed from their
harvest, especially the
olio d'oliva of Tuscany,
is esteemed throughout
the world.*

*Olives grown for curing
and eating are almost
exclusively from Italy's
southern provinces.
Green olives cured
Sicilian style are
prepared in an oily brine
with herbs and garlic.
Tiny, jet black Gaeta
olives, grown around the
gulf and medieval town
of the same name in
southern Lazio, south of
Rome, are the best-
known exceptions to the
southern rule.*

PANE ALLE OLIVE
Olive Bread

◆

MAKES ONE 18-OUNCE LOAF

In *Apulia, Calabria, and Sicily,* la merenda, or *"afternoon snack," is often a hunk of bread and a handful of plump olives. This oval loaf, flecked with bits of Sicilian-style cured green olives, marries bread and salty olives in a single wonderfully crusty package.*

Do not purchase pitted olives for making pane alle olive; *they are tasteless. Removing the pits is no trouble: Just place the olives, one at a time, on a flat, firm surface and smash them once — and decisively — with the heel of your hand. The pits will fly free of the flesh.*

In a small bowl dissolve the yeast in the warm water. Set it aside until it is creamy, about 15 minutes.

Measure the flour into a large bowl. Using a sturdy wooden spoon, stir the salt into the flour. Form a well in the center of the flour mixture and add the yeast mixture, the cool water, and the *biga* to the well. Using the spoon stir together all the ingredients until the dough is too resistant to be stirred.

Knead the dough briefly in the bowl and then turn it out onto a lightly floured work surface and clean off any dough stuck to your hands. Knead vigorously until it is smooth and elastic, about 20 minutes, including some 1- to 2-minute rest periods along the way. The dough is fairly dry at this stage, which makes it relatively easy to knead.

Return the dough to the bowl and add the olives. Gently but firmly knead the olives into the

dough until they are evenly distributed. This will take about 5 minutes. The moistness of the olives makes them want to pop out of the dough; continue kneading gently and the dough will come together beautifully. Shape the dough into a ball.

Rub a large bowl with olive oil and place the dough in the bowl. Turn the ball so that the surface is coated with oil. Cover the bowl with a towel and let the dough rise at room temperature until doubled, about 1½ hours.

Punch down the dough by folding the edges into the center and turning it over so the top is once again smooth. Re-cover the bowl and let the dough rise a second time until doubled, about 45 minutes.

Turn the dough out onto a lightly floured work surface. Trying not to overwork the dough, fold the edges in toward the center. Work in a circular motion, folding the entire rim of the dough in toward the center twice to form a loose round ball with a smooth side.

Place the ball, rough side up, on the floured surface. Using your fingertips gently press the ball out into a disk about 6 inches in diameter and 1 inch thick. Lift up the far edge of the disk and fold it toward you, to rest on top of the disk, so that only one third of the disk remains uncovered. Lift the folded edge and roll it up toward you until the dough takes on a football shape. When you reach the edge nearest you, using the heel of your hand, press the edge of the roll to the bottom edge of the disk to form a seam.

Turn the loaf so that it rests seam side down on a well-floured work surface. Taper the ends of the loaves by simultaneously rolling and pressing them against the work surface with the palms of your hands. Cover with a towel and let rise at room temperature until doubled, about 50 minutes. The dough is ready when it springs back gently upon being lightly pressed with your index finger. Meanwhile, place a baking stone in an oven and preheat to 425 degrees F.

Mist the preheated oven with a spray bottle and quickly shut the oven door. Dust a baker's peel with cornmeal. Gently transfer the loaf to the peel. Using a sharp serrated knife, make 1 slash about ½ inch deep the length of the loaf. Then make 3 diagonal slashes to either side of the slash. Mist the loaf. With a rhythmic snap of the wrist, slide the loaf onto the baking stone. Mist the oven again and bake until the loaf is golden brown on top, dark brown on the bottom, and has a hollow ring when tapped on the bottom, 40 to 50 minutes. Remove to a wire rack to cool completely.

PANINI ALLE OLIVE *Olive Rolls.* Prepare the dough as directed for *pane alle olive* to the point where it is formed into a loaf. Divide the dough into nine 2-ounce portions. Form each portion into a ball by rolling each small piece of dough between your cupped hand and a flour-dusted work surface. As each ball is formed, shape it into a round roll by folding the edges into the center. Work in a circular motion, folding the entire rim of the dough in toward the center several times to form a round ball with a smooth side.

Spread a fairly thick layer of flour on a work surface. Place the rolls, rough sides down, on the flour. Cover with a towel and let rise at room temperature until doubled, about 40 minutes. Following the directions for the loaf, preheat a baking stone in a 425 degree F oven and load the rolls onto a cornmeal-dusted baker's peel. Using a sharp serrated knife, make a single 1-inch-long slash about ½ inch deep in the top of each roll. Then slide the rolls onto the baking stone, remembering to mist the rolls and to mist the oven before and just after putting the rolls into it. Bake until the rolls are golden brown and have a hollow ring when tapped on the bottom, 20 to 30 minutes. Cool on wire racks. Makes nine 2-ounce rolls.

¾ teaspoon active dry yeast

½ cup warm water (105 degrees F)

2¾ cups unbleached bread flour

¾ teaspoon salt

½ cup cool water

¼ cup Biga (page 32)

Additional flour for work surface

½ cup chopped pitted Sicilian-style green olives

Olive oil for bowl

Medium-grind yellow cornmeal for baker's peel

PANMARINO
Rosemary Bread

◆

MAKES ONE 18-OUNCE LOAF

Il *Fornaio created this recipe as a way of bringing one of Italy's most popular herbs into the panificio. The bread, which has a tender white interior flecked with bits of rosemary's distinctive needlelike leaves, is topped with a sprinkling of coarse salt. Sometimes we shape the dough into an oval and mark it with a single slash. Other times we bake a round loaf and slash a starburst pattern in the top. Experiment with creating both shapes.*

The bakery's customers usually buy our rosemary bread for making sandwiches. It complements such fillings as cold roast pork and caramelized onions or grilled eggplant and tangy goat cheese. This fragrant bread uses the same basic dough as pane alle olive, with milk and rosemary added in place of the olives.

◆ ◆ ◆

ROSEMARY
REVERIES

◆

Before I came to work at Il Fornaio, I had never heard of rosemary bread. Of course, the herb itself is as Italian as a Verdi opera and is used in kitchens throughout Italy — tied to a pork loin, a suckling pig, or a veal roast, as a seasoning in risotto or chick-pea and pasta soup, strung on a spit alongside small birds for roasting.

Rosemary mates well with chicken, and at home I use it in pollo a forno. I tuck a couple of pancetta slices, some garlic cloves, half a lemon, and a small handful of rosemary sprigs in the cavity of a chicken, and then strew a few sprigs over the outside of the bird, too. If I am lucky enough to have some chicken left over the next day, it is delicious sandwiched between slices of panmarino.

Prepare the dough for *pane alle olive* through the kneading, omitting the olives as noted.

Return the dough to the bowl and add the rosemary and milk. Gently knead them into the dough until they are completely incorporated, about 5 minutes. As with the olive bread, do not worry if the dough loses its cohesiveness; it is only temporary. Shape the dough into a ball.

Now proceed as for *pane alle olive*, rubbing a bowl with olive oil, placing the dough into it, letting it rise, punching it down, and letting it rise a second time.

Then form the dough into a football-shaped loaf and taper the ends as described for *pane alle olive*. Cover the loaf with a towel and let rise at room temperature for about 50 minutes. The dough is ready when it springs back gently upon being lightly pressed with your index finger. Meanwhile, place a baking stone in an oven and preheat to 425 degrees F.

Mist the preheated oven with a spray bottle and quickly shut the oven door. Dust a baker's peel with cornmeal. Gently transfer the loaf to the peel. Using a sharp serrated knife, make I slash about ½ inch deep the length of the loaf. Sprinkle some coarse sea salt into the slash. With a rhythmic snap of the wrist, slide the loaf onto the baking stone. Mist the oven again and bake until the loaf is golden brown on top, dark brown on the bottom, and has a hollow ring when tapped on the bottom, 40 to 50 minutes. Remove to a wire rack to cool completely.

PANINI MARINO *Rosemary Rolls.* Prepare the dough as directed for *panmarino* to the point where it is formed into a loaf. Divide the dough into nine 2-ounce portions. Form each portion into a ball by rolling each small piece of dough between your cupped hand and a flour-dusted work surface. As each ball is formed, shape it into a round roll by folding the edges into the center. Work in a circular motion, folding the entire rim of the dough in toward the center several times to form a round ball with a smooth side.

Spread a fairly thick layer of flour on a work surface. Place the rolls, rough sides down, on the flour. Cover with a towel and let rise at room temperature until doubled, about 40 minutes. Following the directions for the loaf, preheat a baking stone in a 425 degree F oven and load the rolls onto a cornmeal-dusted baker's peel. Using a sharp serrated knife, make a single I-inch-long slash about ½ inch deep in the top of each roll and sprinkle some coarse sea salt into each slash. Then slide the rolls onto the baking stone, remembering to mist the rolls and to mist the oven before and just after putting the rolls into it. Bake until the rolls are golden brown and have a hollow ring when tapped on the bottom, 20 to 30 minutes. Cool on wire racks. Makes nine 2-ounce rolls.

1 recipe Pane alle Olive dough omitting the olives (page 58)

2 teaspoons roughly chopped fresh rosemary

2 tablespoons milk

Olive oil for bowl

Unbleached bread flour for work surface

Medium-grind yellow cornmeal for baker's peel

Coarse sea salt

PANE ALLE NOCI
Walnut Bread

◆

MAKES TWO 1 1/4-POUND LOAVES

This recipe is basically American in spirit, although it also belongs to la nuova cucina, *the new Italian cooking of the last decade or so. The tradition-bound bakers of my hometown would never think of making walnut bread, however, even though they regularly crack walnuts and eat them along with bread for dessert.*

At Il Fornaio we make pane alle noci *in a handsome double-armed mixer that slowly but surely works our high-protein whole-wheat flour, which is milled from the finest Montana wheat. We use two different whole-wheat flours — a coarse stone-ground type and a finely ground version — in addition to unbleached bread flour. This recipe calls for regular whole-wheat flour, which is the easiest to find in the market, but you may want to experiment with different grinds. You can also divide the dough in half and make one loaf and use the remaining dough to make rolls (directions follow), or you can make two smaller loaves of just one pound each and make six rolls with the leftover dough.*

Walnut bread is wonderful served with a salad or cheese course or sliced and toasted for breakfast.

In a small bowl dissolve the yeast in the warm water. Set it aside until it is creamy, about 15 minutes.

Measure the flours into a large bowl. Using a sturdy wooden spoon, stir the salt into the flours. Form a well in the center of the flour mixture and add the yeast mixture, honey, cool water, and *biga* to the well. Using the spoon stir together all the ingredients until the dough is too resistant to be stirred.

Now begin kneading the dough in the bowl, keeping one hand clean in order to hold and turn the bowl and using the other hand to work the dough. Vigorously fold the dough from the sides of the bowl toward the center, rotating the bowl as you work. Pick up the dough and slap it back into the bowl several times and keep kneading vigorously until the dough comes away cleanly from the sides of the bowl. This should take about 3 minutes.

Turn the dough out onto a lightly floured work surface. Clean off any dough stuck to your hands and then knead the dough until it is smooth and velvety. This will take about 20 minutes, including some 1- to 2-minute rest periods.

On the floured work surface, press the dough out into a disk about 6 inches in diameter and 1 inch thick. Spread the walnuts evenly over the surface. Fold the disk edge farthest from you toward you, to form a half circle. Beginning at the curved side, roll up the half circle into a log. Then, starting at one end, roll up the log. You

will end up with a large, uneven ball. Now gently knead the nuts into the dough until they are evenly distributed, 5 to 8 minutes. Let the dough rest for a minute or so once or twice during the kneading; it needs to relax a little so that the nuts do not pop out. Shape the dough into a ball.

Rub a large bowl with olive oil and place the ball in the bowl. Turn the ball so that the surface is coated with oil. Cover the bowl with a towel and let the dough rise at room temperature until doubled, about 1 hour.

Punch down the dough by folding the edges into the center and turning it over so the top is once again smooth. Press most but not all of the air out of the dough. Re-cover the bowl and let the dough rise at room temperature a second time until doubled, 45 minutes to 1 hour.

Turn the dough out onto a lightly floured work surface. Divide the dough into 2 equal portions. Working with 1 portion at a time, fold the edges in toward the center. Work in a circular motion, folding the entire rim of the dough in toward the center several times to form a round ball with a smooth side.

Place the loaf, rough side down, on a floured surface. Taper the ends of the loaf by simultaneously rolling and pressing them against the work surface with the palms of your hands. Shape the remaining dough into a second loaf in the same

2 teaspoons active dry yeast

½ cup warm water (105 degrees F)

3¼ cups whole-wheat flour

3¼ cups unbleached bread flour

1 tablespoon salt

1 tablespoon honey

2¼ cups cool water

½ cup Biga (page 32)

Additional bread flour for work surface

1½ cups mixed walnut halves and pieces

Olive oil for bowl

Medium-grind yellow cornmeal for baker's peel

manner. Cover the loaves with a towel and let rise at room temperature until doubled, 40 to 50 minutes. The dough is ready when it springs back gently upon being lightly pressed with your index finger. Meanwhile, place a baking stone in an oven and preheat to 425 degrees F.

Mist the preheated oven with a spray bottle and quickly shut the oven door. Dust a baker's peel with cornmeal. Gently slip your hand under each loaf and slip it onto the peel. Using a sharp serrated knife, make I slash about ½ inch deep the length of each loaf. Mist the loaves. With a rhythmic snap of the wrist, slide the loaves onto the baking stone. Mist the oven again and bake the breads for 5 minutes. Mist one more time and bake until the loaves are dark brown and have a hollow ring when tapped on the bottom, 45 to 55 minutes. Remove to wire racks to cool completely.

PANINI ALLE NOCI *Walnut Rolls.* Prepare the dough as directed for *pane alle noci* to the point where it is formed into loaves. Divide the dough into twenty-four 2-ounce portions. Form each portion into a ball by rolling it between your cupped hand and a flour-dusted work surface. As each ball is formed, shape it into a round roll by folding the edges in toward the center in the same manner as for the loaves.

Following the directions for the loaves, place the rolls, smooth sides up, on a floured surface, let them rise, and load them onto the cornmeal-dusted baker's peel. Using a sharp serrated knife make a single, ½-inch-deep diagonal slash in the top of each roll and mist the rolls. With a rhythmic snap of the wrist, slide the rolls onto a baking stone in an oven preheated to 425 degrees F. (Introduce the rolls into the oven in two batches, as it is difficult to slide all 24 rolls onto the stone at once.) Remember to mist the oven before and immediately after putting the rolls into it. Bake for 5 minutes, mist again, and bake until the rolls are dark brown and have a hollow ring when tapped on the bottom, about 30 minutes. Cool on wire racks. Makes twenty-four 2-ounce rolls.

◆　◆　◆

PANE ALL'UVA
Raisin Bread

───────────────◆───────────────

MAKES TWO 1-POUND LOAVES

The Il Fornaio bakers make this bread with a high proportion of raisins, and once you have mastered the recipe, I encourage you to increase the amount called for here. This bread is heartier than the conventional American raisin loaf and is sweeter because of the use of golden raisins. Try shaping just one loaf and using the remaining dough to make small disk-shaped rolls (directions follow). Both the bread and the rolls are wonderful toasted and spread with sweet butter.

THE HIGH COST OF RAISINS

◆

In California we think of raisins as being quite ordinary, because they are produced in such great numbers and exported all over the world. The Golden State owes its international raisin reputation to that celebrated son of Genoa, Christopher Columbus, who, on his second voyage to the New World in 1493, carried in the holds of his vessels the means to cultivate grapes as well as many other Old World plants.

If you travel through Italy, you will see grapevines everywhere. Why, then, are raisins so relatively costly in the land of Columbus? In a word, thirst. It is difficult for Italians to "waste" a grape by drying it, when it could be pressed for making their beloved wine.

Place the raisins in a bowl and add water to cover. Let stand for 2 hours.

Begin making the dough after the raisins have been soaking for about 1½ hours. In a small bowl dissolve the yeast in the warm water. Set it aside until it is creamy, about 15 minutes.

Measure the flour into a large bowl. Using a sturdy wooden spoon, stir the salt into the flour. Form a well in the center of the flour mixture and add the yeast mixture, cool water, olive oil, and *biga* to the well. Using the spoon stir together all the ingredients until the dough is too resistant to be stirred.

Now begin kneading the dough in the bowl, keeping one hand clean in order to hold and turn the bowl and using the other hand to work the dough. Vigorously fold the dough from the sides of the bowl toward the center, rotating the bowl as you work. Pick up the dough and slap it back into the bowl several times and keep kneading vigorously until the dough comes away cleanly from the sides of the bowl. This should take about 5 minutes.

Turn the dough out onto a lightly floured work surface. Clean off any dough stuck to your hands and then knead the dough until it is smooth, 15 to 20 minutes.

Return the dough to the bowl. Drain the raisins well and add them to the dough. Gently but firmly knead the raisins into the dough until they are evenly distributed. This will take up to 10 minutes. Do not be alarmed if the dough seems to fall apart; the moisture in the raisins causes this to happen. As you continue to knead, the dough will come together again beautifully. Shape the dough into a ball.

Rub a large bowl with olive oil and place the dough in the bowl. Turn the ball so that the surface is coated with oil. Cover the bowl with a towel and let the dough rise at room temperature until doubled, about 1 hour.

Punch down the dough by folding the edges into the center and turning it over so the top is once again smooth. Press most but not all of the air out of the dough. Re-cover the bowl and let the dough rise at room temperature a second time until doubled, about 45 minutes.

Turn the dough out onto a lightly floured work surface. Divide the dough into 2 equal portions. Working with 1 portion at a time, fold the edges in toward the center. Work in a circular motion, folding the entire rim of the dough in toward the center several times to form a round ball with a smooth side.

Place the loaf, rough side down, on a floured surface. Taper the ends of the loaf by simultaneously rolling and pressing them against the work surface with the palms of your hands. Shape the remaining dough into a second loaf in the same manner. Cover the loaves with a towel and let rise at room temperature until doubled, 40 to 50 minutes. Meanwhile, place a baking stone in an oven and preheat to 425 degrees F.

Mist the preheated oven with a spray bottle and quickly shut the oven door. Dust a baker's peel with cornmeal. Brush each loaf generously with olive oil, then gently slip your hand under each loaf and slip it onto the peel. With a rhythmic snap of the wrist, slide the loaves onto the baking stone. Mist the oven again and bake the breads for 5 minutes. Mist one more time and bake until the raisins on top are very dark and the loaves are a deep golden brown and have a hollow ring when tapped on the bottom, 50 minutes to 1 hour. Let cool completely on wire racks, then brush again generously with olive oil.

PIADINE ALL'UVA *Raisin Rolls.* Prepare the dough as directed for *pane all'uva* to the point where it is formed into loaves.

Divide the dough into ten 3½-ounce portions. Form each portion into a ball by rolling it between your cupped hand and a flour-dusted work surface. As each ball is formed, place it on a floured surface. Cover with a towel and let rise at room temperature until doubled, about 50 minutes.

Gently press enough air out of each ball to form a disk about 2½ inches in diameter and ¾ inch thick. Generously brush the disks with olive oil. Following the directions for the loaves, load the disks onto the cornmeal-dusted baker's peel and with a rhythmic snap of the wrist, slide the disks onto a baking stone in an oven preheated to 425 degrees F. Remember to mist the oven before and immediately after putting the disks into it. Bake for 5 minutes, mist again, and then bake until the raisins on top are very dark and the disks are golden brown and have a hollow ring when tapped on the bottom, 20 to 30 minutes. Cool on wire racks, then brush again generously with olive oil. Makes ten 3½-ounce flat rolls.

1¼ cups golden raisins

1 tablespoon active dry yeast

½ cup warm water (105 degrees F)

4 cups unbleached bread flour

½ teaspoon salt

1 cup cool water

1 tablespoon extra-virgin olive oil

2 tablespoons Biga (page 32)

Additional flour for work surface

Additional olive oil for bowl and loaves

Medium-grind yellow cornmeal for baker's peel

PANE ALLE PATATE

Potato Bread

MAKES ONE 18-OUNCE LOAF

This dough will not "develop" in the same way as most bread doughs because it is essentially one part flour to one part potatoes. But it requires less kneading, too — about ten minutes will produce sufficient gluten for this loaf to rise beautifully. Bread dough made with potato results in a softer crust than all-flour doughs, which means the loaf stays fresh for two or three days. This bread has a smooth, rich interior that complements roasted meats or grilled salmon, and makes an outstanding sandwich base for grilled vegetables.

◆　◆　◆

Potatoes are indigenous to South America's towering Andes, which made it possible to plant them successfully in the harsh mountainous stretches of the Valle d'Aosta in northern Italy and Basilicata in the south. In Lombardy and the Veneto, gnocchi di patate and patate al forno are common fare; in the Abruzzi potatoes are traditionally roasted beneath a blanket of hot coals.

Whenever my mother makes soup, she always starts out by adding two or three potatoes to the water, to flavor and thicken the zuppa. She also believes in the curative power of the potato skin. When I was a boy and came down with an adolescent toothache, my mother would wrap potato skins in a napkin and tell me to hold the simple compress against my throbbing jaw. Somehow the skins magically absorbed the flame of the pain.

In a small bowl dissolve the yeast in the warm water. Set it aside until it is creamy, about 15 minutes.

Place the cooked potatoes in a large mixing bowl and mash them well with the back of a sturdy wooden spoon. Measure the mashed potatoes and return 1½ cups to the bowl to use for the bread dough; reserve any remaining potato for another use. Add the flour, salt, olive oil, garlic, parsley, and *biga* to the bowl. Now begin kneading the dough in the bowl, keeping one hand clean in order to hold and turn the bowl and using the other to work the dough.

As soon as the mixture comes together in a rough yet cohesive mass, which will happen rather quickly, add the yeast mixture and continue to knead the dough in the bowl. Vigorously fold the dough from the sides of the bowl toward the center, rotating the bowl as you work. Pick up the dough and slap it back into the bowl several times and keep kneading vigorously until it is tender and somewhat smooth, about 10 minutes. Shape the dough into a ball.

Rub a large bowl with olive oil and place the dough in the bowl. Turn the ball so that the surface is coated with oil. Cover the bowl with a towel and let the dough rise at room temperature until doubled, about 1¼ hours.

Punch down the dough by folding the edges into the center and turning it over so the top is once again smooth. Re-cover the bowl and let the dough rise a second time until doubled, about 45 minutes.

Turn the dough out onto a lightly floured work surface. Trying not to overwork the dough, fold the edges in toward the center. Work in a circular motion, folding the entire rim of the dough in toward the center several times to form a round ball with a smooth side.

Spread a fairly thick layer of flour on a work surface. Place the ball of dough, rough side down, on the flour. Cover the loaf with a towel and let rise at room temperature for about 50 minutes. The dough is ready when it springs back gently upon being lightly pressed with your index finger. Meanwhile, place a baking stone in an oven and preheat to 425 degrees F.

Mist the preheated oven with a spray bottle and quickly shut the oven door. Dust a baker's peel with cornmeal. Gently slip your hand under the loaf and turn it over onto the peel. There should be a fairly thick coating of flour on the top. Mist the loaf. With a rhythmic snap of the wrist, slide the loaf onto the baking stone. Mist the oven again and bake the bread for 5 minutes. Mist one more time and bake the loaf until it is golden brown on top, dark brown on the bottom, and has a hollow ring when tapped on the bottom, 40 to 50 minutes. Remove to a wire rack to cool completely.

1 teaspoon active dry yeast

½ cup warm water (105 degrees F)

2 medium baking potatoes, boiled in water to cover until tender, drained, peeled, and cooled to room temperature

2 cups unbleached bread flour

½ teaspoon salt

1 tablespoon extra-virgin olive oil

¼ teaspoon minced garlic

2 tablespoons minced fresh parsley

¼ cup Biga (page 32)

Additional olive oil for bowl

Additional flour for work surface

Medium-grind yellow cornmeal for baker's peel

TWO TALES OF
PANETTONE

◆

There are many stories
as to the origin of
Milan's majestic
panettone, among them
two very different tales.
The first suggests that its
tall, cylindrical shape
was created to honor the
towers of Milan's great
Duomo. The second
claims that it was the
invention of a clever
fornaio named Tonio,
who proudly named it
"the bread of Tony."

Christmas is not
Christmas in Italy
without panettone.
Large Italian food
operations such as
Alemagna and Motta
bake hundreds of
thousands of these
traditional breads for
shipment all over the
country — and the world.
In the past a ritual
always attended the
cutting of this celebratory
loaf. Each family
member took a taste
from each of the first
three slices to ensure luck
in the future.

PANETTONE
Egg Bread with Raisins and Candied Fruit

MAKES ONE 1 1/2-POUND LOAF

Baking a panettone is like baking a soufflé. It rises gloriously in the oven and then deflates as it cools. Our Il Fornaio bakers were at a loss as to what to do about the fallen loaves, so I introduced them to the foolproof Italian remedy: Italian bakers suspend boards pierced by a row of round holes from the ceiling. As they take the breads from the hot oven, they drop them upside down through the holes. The loaves' slightly broader bases prevent them from slipping all the way through and the breads retain their full height as they cool.

Making this handsome, fruit-studded Christmas bread — with the dough's four long resting periods — is an all-day event. Ideally the loaves are baked in high-sided panettone molds, but they are difficult to find on this side of the Atlantic. If you are not planning a trip to Italy before Christmas, use a two-pound coffee can or a two-quart charlotte mold or soufflé dish. This loaf tastes best the day after it is baked, so plan ahead.

◆ ◆ ◆

To make the starter, in a small bowl stir the yeast into the water. Add the flour and mix vigorously with a wooden spoon for 5 minutes to form a smooth batter. Top with an airtight cover and let rest at room temperature until doubled, 30 minutes to 1 hour.

Once the starter is ready, begin to make the first dough. In a mixing bowl combine the butter and sugar and beat together with a sturdy wooden spoon until light, about 2 minutes. Add the egg and beat until incorporated. Stir in the risen starter, which will deflate immediately, and beat until smooth. Gradually stir in the flour and mix vigorously for 3 to 4 minutes. At this point the dough should be somewhat stiff and sticky, but nonetheless smooth and elastic. Once again top with an airtight cover and let rise until doubled, 3 to 5 hours.

Transfer the now-risen first dough to a large mixing bowl. It will deflate as you do. Now begin to make the second dough. In a smaller bowl combine the butter and sugar. Using a hand-held mixer set on medium speed, beat the mixture until light, about 2 minutes. Add the whole egg and egg yolks and beat until thoroughly combined. Add the vanilla, honey, salt, and citrus zests and beat only until evenly mixed.

Using a wooden spoon, beat the egg mixture into the first dough and continue to beat until smooth. Add the candied citrus rinds and raisins and beat to distribute evenly, about 1 minute. Stir in 1 cup of the flour.

Turn the dough out onto a lightly floured work surface. Knead the dough, gradually adding more flour as necessary to achieve a soft, very smooth, elastic dough. This should take 5 to 7 minutes. Shape the dough into a ball.

Rub a large bowl with oil and place the dough in the bowl. Turn the ball so that the surface is coated with oil. Top the bowl with an airtight cover and let the dough rise at room temperature until tripled, 3 to 5 hours.

Grease the bread mold (see recipe introduction) with butter and dust with flour. Cut out a round of parchment paper to fit the mold bottom precisely and slip it into place. Punch down the dough by loosely folding the edges into the center and turning it over so the top is once again smooth. Do not press all of the air out as you shape it into a loose ball. Place the ball in the prepared mold. Using a sharp serrated knife, cut a ½-inch-deep X in the top of the loaf, extending it to the edges. Cover the mold with a damp towel (the towel must be damp because the dough is very sticky) and let the loaf rise at room temperature until doubled, 2½ to 4 hours.

Preheat an oven to 400 degrees F. Cut a second X in the top of the loaf, retracing the lines of the first X. Bake the loaf in the preheated oven for 10 minutes. Reduce the oven temperature to 350 degrees F and bake until a cake tester or a thin bamboo skewer inserted in the center comes out dry, about 40 minutes longer. Remove to a wire rack to cool in the mold for 30 minutes. Then gently slide the loaf out of the mold and cool it on its side, giving it a quarter turn every 10 to 15 minutes, until cooled completely. To store, wrap tightly and keep at room temperature for up to 3 days.

For the starter:

2 teaspoons active dry yeast
½ cup warm water (105 degrees F)
½ cup unbleached all-purpose flour

For the first dough:

2 tablespoons unsalted butter, at room temperature
4 teaspoons sugar
1 egg
The starter
⅔ cup unbleached all-purpose flour

For the second dough:

4 tablespoons unsalted butter, at room temperature
¼ cup sugar
1 whole egg
2 eggs yolks
1 teaspoon vanilla extract
2 teaspoons honey
Pinch of salt
Grated zest of 1 orange
Grated zest of 1 lemon
2 tablespoons chopped candied orange rind
2 tablespoons chopped candied lemon rind
½ cup raisins, soaked in hot water to cover for 30 minutes and drained
1 to 1½ cups unbleached all-purpose flour

Additional flour for work surface and mold
Olive oil for bowl
Additional unsalted butter for mold

COLOMBA PASQUALE
Easter Dove Bread

◆

MAKES ONE 1 1/2-POUND LOAF

History records that Milanese bakers created colomba pasquale *following the appearance in their city of two heaven-sent doves celebrating Milan's defeat of the Emperor Frederick Barbarossa in the twelfth century. Contemporary bakers achieve the unique dove shape by baking this cakelike bread in a paper form. But because the paper forms are difficult to locate, this loaf is shaped by hand.*

Prepare the dough for *panettone* through the rising of the second dough, omitting the ingredients noted and, as directed, increasing the candied orange rind to ⅔ cup.

Line a baking sheet with parchment paper or grease it with butter. On a lightly floured work surface, divide the dough into 2 equal portions. Using the palms of your hands, roll out one portion into a log about 7 inches long and 1½ inches in diameter. Lay the log crosswise on the prepared baking sheet at about the midpoint, and flatten to a thickness of about ¾ inch. This log is the wings of the dove. Now form the second portion into a 10-inch log in the same manner. Taper one end to form the head and flatten the other end to form the tail. Lay this log atop the first log so that it runs lengthwise down the center of the pan and the "wings" extend to either side of it. Flatten this log only slightly. Cover with a damp towel and let rise at room temperature until doubled, 2½ to 4 hours.

Preheat an oven to 400 degrees F. Uncover the dove and then make the topping. Set 10

almonds aside. Using a nut mill, blender, or a food processor fitted with the metal blade, grind the almonds to a fine powder. (If you are using a blender or food processor, grind them with the granulated sugar in small batches to keep them from releasing too much oil. If the nuts do become oily, pass them through a sieve to break up any lumps.) Transfer to a small bowl and stir in the granulated sugar. Then lightly whisk in enough of the egg white to make a brushable glaze that is not too thin. Using a pastry brush, gently paint the dove all over with the almond mixture, being careful not to deflate the dough. Place the whole almonds in a cross pattern on the top. Sprinkle with the turbinado sugar and then sieve the powdered sugar over the top.

Bake the loaf in the preheated oven for 10 minutes. Reduce the oven temperature to 350 degrees F and bake until golden brown, 25 to 35 minutes longer. Using 2 spatulas, transfer the dove to a wire rack to cool completely. The bread tastes best a day after baking. To store, wrap well and keep at room temperature for up to 3 days.

1 recipe Panettone dough omitting the lemon zest, candied lemon rind, and raisins and increasing the candied orange rind to ⅔ cup diced rind (page 70)

Unsalted butter for baking sheet (optional)

Unbleached all-purpose flour for work surface

For the topping:

½ cup blanched whole almonds

¼ cup granulated sugar

1 to 2 egg whites

2 tablespoons turbinado sugar

Powdered sugar for dusting

PANE DI NOVE CEREALI

Nine-Grain Bread

❖

MAKES ONE 1 1/4-POUND LOAF

When Il Fornaio premiered this bread, it contained only seven cereals. Not long after, the number grew to nine, no doubt in response to Americans' growing concerns about wholesome eating. In Italy there is less interest in so-called health foods, and theories about how to diet can be very different, too. Perhaps the philosophy has changed, but in the past when the women of my town wanted to lose weight, they went on a "white diet." No prosciutto, salami, or spicy food was allowed. Instead they ate "white" only — butter, cheese, yogurt, chicken breast, veal, pasta al burro e parmigiano. Not an unpleasant regimen.

At Il Fornaio we use a cereal that combines cracked wheat, barley, oats, corn, rye, millet, triticale, brown rice, and flax. Any uncooked, unsweetened multigrain cereal can be used, however.

❖ ❖ ❖

THE GENTRIFICATION OF CORN

❖

Lombardians are the premier growers of granturco ("corn") in Italy. Nearly every family in the region has a tall, narrow copper pot reserved solely for cooking polenta. Cornmeal also goes into Lombardian bread and cookie doughs and into cake batters.

But corn was not always so highly appreciated by all the classes. Throughout much of the seventeenth century, corn in any form was thought of as peasant fare (and even today is eaten regularly only in the north). Most culinary scholars agree that its acceptance by the upper classes owes much to two authors, eighteenth-century poet Domenica Battachi and nineteenth-century novelist Alessandro Manzoni, both of whom recounted the preparation of polenta in their widely admired works.

Place the cereal in a small bowl and pour ½ cup of the cool water over the top. Set aside for 1 hour.

In a small bowl dissolve the yeast in the warm water. Set it aside until it is creamy, about 15 minutes.

Measure the flours into a large bowl. Using a sturdy wooden spoon, stir the salt into the flours. Form a well in the center of the flour mixture and add the yeast mixture, the remaining ½ cup cool water, the olive oil, the honey, and the cereal mixture to the well. Using the spoon stir together all the ingredients until the dough is too resistant to be stirred.

Knead the dough briefly in the bowl and then turn it out onto a lightly floured work surface. Clean off any dough stuck to your hands and then knead the dough until it is smooth and elastic. This will take 15 to 20 minutes, including some 1- to 2-minute rest periods. Shape the dough into a ball.

Rub a large bowl with olive oil and place the dough in the bowl. Turn the ball so that the surface is coated with oil. Cover the bowl with a towel and let the dough rise at room temperature until doubled, about 1 hour.

Punch down the dough by folding the edges into the center and turning it over so the top is once again smooth. Re-cover the bowl and let the dough rise a second time until doubled, about 45 minutes.

Turn the dough out onto a lightly floured work surface. Trying not to overwork the dough, fold the edges in toward the center. Work in a circular motion, folding the entire rim of the dough in toward the center several times to form a round ball with a smooth side. Spread the rolled oats out on a work surface. Mist the loaf lightly with a spray bottle and roll the smooth top and sides of the loaf in the oats to cover completely (leave the rough bottom uncovered).

Spread a fairly thick layer of flour on a work surface. Place the ball of dough, rough side down, on the flour. Cover the loaf with a towel and let rise at room temperature until doubled, 40 to 50 minutes. The dough is ready when it springs back gently upon being lightly pressed with your index finger. Meanwhile, place a baking stone in an oven and preheat to 400 degrees F.

Mist the preheated oven and quickly shut the oven door. Dust a baker's peel with cornmeal. Gently slip your hand under the loaf and slide it onto the peel. Mist the loaf generously. With a rhythmic snap of the wrist, slide the loaf onto the baking stone. Mist the oven again and bake the bread for 5 minutes. Mist one more time and bake the loaf until it is fairly dark on top and has a hollow ring when tapped on the bottom, about 40 minutes. Remove to a wire rack to cool completely.

½ cup nine-grain cereal

1 cup cool water

¾ teaspoon active dry yeast

½ cup warm water (105 degrees F)

½ cup unbleached bread flour

2½ cups whole-wheat flour

½ teaspoon salt

1 tablespoon extra-virgin olive oil

1 tablespoon honey

Additional bread flour for work surface

Additional olive oil for bowl

½ cup rolled oats

Medium-grind yellow cornmeal for baker's peel

*Perhaps the best-known
Jewish settlement in
Italy is in the
Cannaregio quarter of
Venice. Indeed, it was
the Venetians who coined
the word ghetto — from
their dialect word
gettar, "to cast out" —
for the walled-off area of
the city where Jews were
required to live in the
Middle Ages. According
to Faith Heller Willinger,
in her estimable* Eating
in Italy, *Venice's ghetto
vecchio has a thriving
community baking
facility open each year
only for the month
preceding Passover.*

*On a trip to Tuscany
before I entered hotel
school, I stopped to stay
with a friend in
Pitigliano, long ago
nicknamed Little
Jerusalem. A palazzo
draws some tourists
there, who, if they search
it out, will also discover
Vicolo Manin and its
crumbling synagogue, a
remnant of a once-sizable
Jewish community.*

CHALLAH
Braided Egg Bread

MAKES ONE 1 1/4-POUND LOAF

This classic Jewish egg bread is available at Il Fornaio bakeries in the United States on Friday evenings, the beginning of the Sabbath. In my days at the Panificio d'Alba I recall making a bread similar to challah, which was called chiffer in the local dialect and pane di lusso in Italian. It was dubbed the latter — "luxury bread" — because of the inclusion of eggs.

The traditional challah is formed into a long oval with tapered ends. At Il Fornaio we shape this braided bread into an almost square loaf. Both techniques work equally well. In either case, it is best to bake the loaf on a cornmeal-dusted aluminum baking sheet rather than on a stone, to achieve a thin, light bottom crust.

Jewish children in America like to spread challah with cream cheese and jam instead of the more conventional youngsters' combo of peanut butter and jelly. It is also delectable toasted for breakfast and spread with sweet butter. It will keep well for five days or so.

◆　◆　◆

In a small bowl disolve the yeast in the warm water. Set it aside until it is creamy, about 15 minutes.

Measure the flour into a large bowl. Using a sturdy wooden spoon, stir the salt and sugar into the flour. Form a well in the center of the flour mixture and add the yeast mixture, eggs, oil, and *biga* to the well. Using the spoon stir together all the ingredients until the dough is too resistant to be stirred.

Now begin kneading the dough in the bowl (it will be quite sticky), keeping one hand clean in order to hold and turn the bowl and using the other hand to work the dough. Vigorously fold the dough from the sides of the bowl toward the center, rotating the bowl as you work. Pick up the dough and slap it back into the bowl several times and keep kneading vigorously until the dough comes away cleanly from the sides of the bowl. This should take about 5 minutes.

Turn the dough out onto a lightly floured work surface. Clean off any dough stuck to your hands and then knead the dough until it is smooth and velvety. This will take about 20 minutes, including some 1- to 2-minute rest periods. Shape the dough into a ball.

Rub a large bowl with olive oil and place the ball in the bowl. Turn the ball so that the surface is coated with oil. Cover the bowl with a towel and let the dough rise at room temperature until doubled, about 1½ hours.

Punch down the dough by folding the edges into the center and turning it over so the top is once again smooth. Press most but not all of the air out of the dough. Re-cover the bowl and let the dough rise at room temperature a second time until doubled, about 45 minutes.

Turn the dough out onto a lightly floured work surface. Divide the dough into 3 equal portions. Working with 1 portion at a time and using the palms of your hands, roll it into a "strand" about 12 inches long and 1 inch in diameter. Repeat with the 2 remaining portions. Braid these 3 strands together, just as you would braid hair. Once the braid is formed, you may, if you like, taper the ends of the loaf by gently pulling the strands on either end. Pinch the ends together to seal securely and then roll them between your palms to smooth them.

Place the loaf on a well-floured surface. Cover with a towel and let rise at room temperature until doubled, 50 to 60 minutes. Meanwhile, preheat an oven to 400 degrees F.

Mist the preheated oven with a spray bottle and quickly shut the oven door. Dust an aluminum baking sheet with cornmeal. Gently slip your hand under the loaf and transfer it to the peel. For the topping, in a small bowl whisk together the egg and water and brush it on top of the loaf. Immediately sprinkle the loaf with the sesame seeds. Place the baking sheet in the oven. Mist the oven again and bake the bread for 5 minutes. Mist one more time and bake until the loaf is golden brown and has a hollow ring when tapped on the bottom, 30 to 40 minutes. Remove to a wire rack to cool completely.

½ teaspoon active dry yeast

½ cup warm water (105 degrees F)

2½ cups unbleached bread flour

½ teaspoon salt

2 tablespoons sugar

2 medium eggs

¼ cup extra-virgin olive oil

¼ cup Biga (page 32)

Additional flour for work surface

Additional olive oil for bowl

Medium-grind yellow cornmeal for baking sheet

For the topping:

1 small egg

1 tablespoon water

2 tablespoons sesame seeds

PANINI

Little Breads

MAGGIOLINI
Oblong Rolls 84

❖

PANINI DEL FORNAIO
Square Rolls 86

❖

GRISSINI TORINESI
Breadsticks from Turin 88

❖

FOCACCETTE ALLE CIPOLLE
Onion Rolls 90

❖

FOCACCETTE AL ROSMARINO
Rosemary Rolls 91

❖

PANE DEL PESCATORE
Fisherman's Bread 93

There are an infinite number of names and shapes for *panini* in Italy, all of them a source of great regional pride. It is also not unusual to find two towns calling essentially the same roll by two different names. For example, the Emilian *montasu*, scroll-shaped *panini* in which one end of the scroll is twisted and placed at an angle atop the other, is called a *pirlinc* in Milanese dialect. The Milanese *michetta*, on the other hand, is known as a *rosetta* in Florence.

The northerners are the top *panini* eaters, and at the Panificio d'Alba we made seven or eight distinct rolls for our customers. The cornet was the most popular shape, a graceful cylinder that graduated ever so slowly from very narrow to slightly wide. It was the roll I enjoyed making the most. But we also baked some small breads in the form of a hand or a rosette and others that looked like braids or S's or even ladybugs.

I loved loading the small breads onto a baker's peel that was so long and narrow they had to be placed in single file. It took me three or four months to master the snap of the wrist that sent the *panini* into the oven without having them all tumble against the back wall or into the fire. I had not seen one of those skinny peels for years, and then I stopped one day in the small central California town of San Juan Bautista. There, in a bakery on the main square, was an elderly baker using just such a peel; his rolls sailed into the oven without mishap, his fluid movement the grace of a master.

A number of recipes in the chapters on traditional breads and special breads include directions for rolls. The nut- and raisin-loaded doughs in the latter make particularly delicious *panini*.

PANINI

FOCACCETTE AL ROSMARINO   FOCACCETTE ALLE CIPOLLE

GRISSINI TORINESI

Panini

Pane del Pescatore

Panini del Fornaio

Maggiolini

In addition to pastries
and sweet rolls, most
Italian bar-caffè carry
an assortment of
sandwiches, or panini
(the same word is used
for filled and unfilled
rolls). They are
commonly eaten at
mid-morning for a
pick-me-up, at noon
when only a half-hour
lunch is possible, and for
a mid-afternoon snack.
A shop that features
sandwiches is called a
paninoteca, and in
such establishments the
customer finds
everything from a simple
panino di prosciutto
to high-rise creations that
stack meats, vegetables,
fish, and cheeses in a
variety of combinations.
Because northern
Italy is home to many
different small breads, it
is also home to our
foremost sandwich eaters.
Many of these panino
devotees are young people,
who have been
nicknamed paninari.

MAGGIOLINI
Oblong Rolls

MAKES TWELVE 3 1/2-OUNCE ROLLS

A maggiolino is a "ladybug," and these rectangular rolls with a slight cleft down the center resemble the gentle winged beetles. Ladybugs are first seen each year in the greatest number in May — maggio — and they are tiny, which accounts for the use of the Italian diminutive form lino in their name.

These are northern Italian rolls made from a hard dough and finished in the oven to a golden hue. The clefts are formed with a special stamp in bakeries; you can use the edge of your hand or the slender handle of a wooden spoon. Slipping the dough into the refrigerator overnight for a cool fermentation period gives the baked rolls a particularly full flavor and a shelf life of up to four days.

◆　◆　◆

In a small bowl dissolve the yeast in the warm water. Set it aside until it is creamy, about 15 minutes.

Measure the flour into a large bowl. Using a sturdy wooden spoon, stir the salt into the flour. Form a well in the center of the flour mixture and add the yeast mixture, cool water, and *biga*. Using the spoon stir together all the ingredients until the dough is too resistant to be stirred.

Knead the dough briefly in the bowl and then turn it out onto a lightly floured surface. Clean off any dough stuck to your hands, and then knead the dough until it is fairly smooth, about 15 minutes. This is a "dry" dough that will prove easy to handle. Shape the dough into a ball.

Rub a large bowl with olive oil and place the dough in the bowl. Turn the ball so that the surface is coated with oil. Cover the bowl with a towel and let the dough rise at room temperature until doubled, about 1½ hours.

Punch down the dough by folding the edges into the center and turning it over so the top is once again smooth. Press most but not all of the air out of the dough. Cover the bowl tightly and refrigerate overnight for a long, cool fermentation.

Remove from the refrigerator and let rise at room temperature until doubled, about 1 hour. Punch down as before, cover with a towel, and let rise at room temperature again until doubled, about 1 hour.

Turn the dough out onto a lightly floured work surface. Divide the dough into 12 equal portions. Form each portion into a ball by rolling each piece of dough between your cupped hand and a flour-dusted work surface. Press the edge of your hand or the handle of a wooden spoon into the center each ball to form a deep cleft that reaches to within about ¼ inch of the base of the ball.

Place the balls, cleft sides down, on a heavily floured surface. Cover with a towel and let rise until doubled, 35 to 40 minutes. Meanwhile, place a baking stone in an oven and preheat to 425 degrees F.

Mist the preheated oven with a spray bottle and quickly shut the oven door. Dust a baker's peel with cornmeal. Gently transfer the rolls to the peel, turning each roll cleft side up. Mist the rolls. With a rhythmic snap of the wrist, slide them onto the baking stone. Bake the rolls for 5 minutes and then mist the oven again. Continue baking the rolls until they are golden brown and have a hollow ring when tapped on the bottom, about 35 minutes. Remove to wire racks to cool completely.

½ teaspoon active dry yeast

½ cup warm water (105 degrees F)

5 cups unbleached bread flour

2½ teaspoons salt

1½ cups cool water

½ cup Biga (page 32)

Additional flour for work surface

Olive oil for bowl

Medium-grind yellow cornmeal for baker's peel

PANINI DEL FORNAIO
Square Rolls

---

1 recipe Pagnotta *dough (page 34)*

Olive oil for dish

Unbleached bread flour for work surface

Medium-grind yellow cornmeal for baker's peel

A crunchy crust covers these classic white rolls. They are ideal for finishing up the tiny bit of sauce left on the plate after you have eaten your pasta.

If you have not yet mastered the technique for sliding a large batch of rolls successfully from a baker's peel onto a baking stone, load these panini *in two or three batches.*

Prepare the dough for *pagnotta* through the first rising.

Rub a baking dish about 6 inches square (or a rectangular dish of roughly the same size) with a liberal amount of olive oil. Turn the risen dough out into it. With your fingertips press the dough evenly into the dish, making certain that it fits snugly into the corners; it should reach no more than halfway up the sides of the dish. Cover with a towel and let rise at room temperature until doubled, about 1½ hours.

Gently invert the risen dough out onto a well-floured work surface. Divide the dough into 4 equal squares. Working with 1 square at a time and using your fingertips, gently press out most of the air. Fold about ½ inch of the square edge farthest from you toward you. Then continue to roll up the square toward you, in the same manner as you would securely wrap silverware in a cloth napkin. Try to introduce some tension into the roll so that it is fairly tight; it should be about 1½ inches in diameter. When you reach the edge

nearest you, using the heel of your hand, press the edge of the roll to the bottom edge of the square to form a seam. Repeat with the 3 remaining squares.

Turn each roll so that it rests seam side down on a well-floured work surface. Cover with a towel and let rise at room temperature until doubled, about 45 minutes. Meanwhile, place a baking stone in an oven and preheat to 425 degrees F.

Cut each roll crosswise into 5 equal pieces. Let the pieces rest for 10 minutes. Mist the preheated oven with a spray bottle and quickly shut the oven door. Dust a baker's peel with cornmeal. Gently transfer the rolls to the peel and mist the rolls. With a rhythmic snap of the wrist, slide them onto the baking stone. Bake the rolls for 5 minutes and then mist the oven again. Continue baking the rolls until they are golden brown and have a hollow ring when tapped on the bottom, 30 to 35 minutes. Remove to wire racks to cool completely.

GRISSINI TORINESI
Breadsticks from Turin

◆

MAKES ABOUT 3 DOZEN 12-INCH BREADSTICKS

Turin is the home of grissini. These crunchy sticks have spread from there to Italian-restaurant tables from Hong Kong to New York. Breadsticks are for people who love la crosta, *for they are essentially pure crust. (According to the late food historian Waverley Root, Napoleon must have been a crust man, for he is said to have eaten many a grissino, which he called a* batonnet.*)*

The best grissini are friabile, *that is, they crumble when you bite into them. Sometimes you encounter a grissino that is so hard that it seems likely you will break your teeth on it. The only way to consume it safely is to soak it first in soup.*

In a small bowl dissolve the yeast in the warm water. Set it aside until it is creamy, about 15 minutes.

Measure the flour into a large bowl. Using a sturdy wooden spoon, stir the salt into the flour. Form a well in the center of the flour mixture and add the yeast mixture, the cool water, and the *biga* to the well. Using the spoon stir together all the ingredients until the dough is too resistant to be stirred.

Now begin kneading the dough in the bowl, keeping one hand clean in order to hold and turn the bowl and using the other hand to work the dough. Vigorously fold the dough from the sides of the bowl toward the center, rotating the bowl as you work. Pick up the dough and slap it back into the bowl several times and keep kneading vigorously until the dough comes away cleanly from the sides of the bowl. This should take about 3 minutes.

Turn the dough out onto a lightly floured work surface. Clean off any dough stuck to your hands and then knead the dough until it is smooth and velvety. This will take about 20 minutes, including some 1- to 2-minute rest periods along the way.

Return the dough to the bowl. With your hand form a well in the center. Break up the butter into small pieces and add it to the well along with the olive oil. Gently knead the dough until the butter and oil are thoroughly incorporated. The dough will break up, but will come together again after 3 to 5 minutes. Shape the dough into a ball.

THE
BREADSTICK
DEBATE

◆

At least two stories (and probably twenty more!) surround the origin of this slender rod of bread. One school of culinary historians attributes its creation to an eighteenth-century baker known as Grissinaro. A second school does not name the baker, but does say that grissini were first made in the 1660s by a chef in the court of Savoy, who was asked to come up with a remedy for a prince suffering gastrointestinitis. The crusty sticks are reputed to have cured his indigestion.

Rub a large bowl with olive oil and place the dough in the bowl. Turn the ball so that the surface is coated with oil. Cover the bowl with a towel and let the dough rise at room temperature until doubled, about 1 hour.

Turn the dough out onto a well-floured work surface. Using your fingertips gently press out most of the air as you form the dough into a rectangle about 9 inches long and 6 inches wide. Fold about ½ inch of the long edge farthest from you toward you. Then continue to roll up the rectangle toward you, in the same manner as you would wrap silverware in a cloth napkin. Try to introduce some tension into the roll so that it is fairly tight and try to keep it no longer than its original length. It will be a very fat roll when you finish, about 6 inches in diameter. When you reach the edge nearest you, using the heel of your hand, press the edge of the roll to the bottom edge of the rectangle to form a seam.

Rub olive oil on a section of your work surface one and one-half times the size of the roll and place the roll on it. Cover with a towel and let rise at room temperature until doubled, about 1 hour. Meanwhile, preheat an oven, with or without a baking stone, to 425 degrees F.

Have ready 2 baking sheets. Uncover the dough roll and brush it on all sides with oil. Using a sharp serrated knife, cut the dough crosswise into ¼-inch-wide pieces, pulling each piece gently away from the roll as you cut it. Cut several pieces at a time and then form them into breadsticks: With one hand grasp the top and with the other the bottom of each piece, pick it up, and gently move your hands outward and parallel. The piece of dough will begin to stretch easily once it is lifted from the surface and should continue to stretch until it is about 12 inches long. As each piece is stretched, place it crosswise on a baking sheet, spacing the breadsticks about ¾ inch apart. Repeat with the remaining dough.

Mist the breadsticks generously with a spray bottle and place the baking sheets in the preheated oven, one directly on the baking stone, if using. Bake the breadsticks for 5 minutes, and then mist the oven. Continue baking until the breadsticks are golden brown on all sides and feel crisp all the way through, 20 to 25 minutes. Remove to wire racks to cool completely.

GRISSINI AL SESAME *Breadsticks with Sesame Seeds.* Prepare the dough for *Grissini Torinesi* through the point where it is brushed with olive oil. Measure out 1 cup sesame seeds. Drop a generous handful of the seeds along the length of the roll and then, with your fingers, spread the seeds evenly over the entire surface of the roll. Add any remaining seeds to the work surface, then, as you cut the dough, pull the pieces into the excess seeds so that the cut sides of each piece are coated. Continue forming them into breadsticks as described for plain *grissini.*

GRISSINI AL PAPAVERO *Breadsticks with Poppy Seeds.* Prepare as described for *Grissini al Sesame,* substituting 1 cup poppy seeds for the sesame seeds.

1½ teaspoons active dry yeast

½ cup warm water (105 degrees F)

5½ cups unbleached bread flour

2 teaspoons salt

1¾ cups cool water

½ cup Biga (page 32)

Additional flour for work surface

1 tablespoon unsalted butter, at room temperature

1 tablespoon extra-virgin olive oil

Additional olive oil for bowl, work surface, and dough

FOCACCETTE ALLE CIPOLLE
Onion Rolls

◆

At Il Fornaio we mix green and yellow onions into the dough before shaping these dimpled rounds. In Italy bakers scatter paper-thin onion slices atop the rolls and then sprinkle them with Italian sea salt just before slipping them into the oven.

1 recipe Focaccia alla
  Genovese *dough*
  (page 40)

1 tablespoon chopped
  green onion

½ tablespoon chopped
  yellow onion

Olive oil for bowl

*Unbleached bread flour
  for work surface*

*Medium-grind yellow
  cornmeal for baker's
  peel*

*Extra-virgin olive oil
  for rolls*

Prepare the dough for *focaccia* through the kneading.

Return the dough to the bowl in which it was mixed and add the green and yellow onions. Gently but firmly knead the onions into the dough until they are evenly distributed. This will take about 5 minutes. Do not be alarmed if the dough seems to fall apart. As you continue to knead, the dough will come together again beautifully. Shape the dough into a ball.

Rub a large bowl with olive oil and place the dough in the bowl. Turn the ball so that the surface is coated with oil. Cover the bowl with a towel and let the dough rise at room temperature until doubled, about 1½ hours.

Punch down the dough by folding the edges into the center and turning it over so the top is once again smooth. Re-cover the bowl and let the dough rise a second time until doubled, about 45 minutes.

Turn the dough out onto a lightly floured work surface. Divide the dough into 6 equal portions. Form each portion into a ball by rolling each small piece of dough between your cupped hand and a flour-dusted work surface. Cover the balls with a towel and let them rise on the floured surface until doubled, about 30 minutes. Meanwhile, place a baking stone in an oven and preheat to 425 degrees F.

Using your fingertips press out each ball into a disk about 2½ inches in diameter. Cover with a towel and let rise for 15 minutes.

Mist the preheated oven with a spray bottle and quickly shut the oven door. Dust a baker's peel with cornmeal. Using a soft-bristled brush, paint each disk lightly with olive oil. Using your fingertips, press "dimples" all over the surface of the disks; they should be about three quarters the depth of the thickness of the disk. Gently transfer the disks to the peel and mist the disks. With a rhythmic snap of the wrist, slide the disks onto the baking stone. Mist the oven again and bake for 5 minutes. Mist one more time and bake until the rolls are a light golden brown and have a hollow ring when tapped on the bottom, 20 to 25 minutes. Remove to wire racks, brush with olive oil, and let cool completely.

FOCACCETTE AL ROSMARINO
Rosemary Rolls

Bakers in Genoa's medieval streets traditionally make their focaccia in great sheets that they carve up into squares for customers. At Il Fornaio we add rosemary to the classic dough and form it into three-inch flat rounds to satisfy the American sandwich lover. Fill the rolls with smoked salmon, mozzarella, and red onions, or use them as stand-ins for hamburger buns.

1 recipe Focaccia alla Genovese *dough* (page 40)

2¼ teaspoons roughly chopped fresh rosemary

Olive oil for bowl

Unbleached bread flour for work surface

Medium-grind yellow cornmeal for baker's peel

Extra-virgin olive oil for rolls

Prepare the dough for *focaccia* through the kneading.

Return the dough to the bowl in which it was mixed and add the rosemary. Gently but firmly knead the rosemary into the dough until it is evenly distributed. This will take about 5 minutes. Do not be alarmed if the dough seems to fall apart. As you continue to knead, the dough will come together again beautifully. Shape the dough into a ball.

Rub a large bowl with olive oil and place the dough in the bowl. Turn the ball so that the surface is coated with oil. Cover the bowl with a towel and let the dough rise at room temperature until doubled, about 1½ hours.

Punch down the dough by folding the edges into the center and turning it over so the top is once again smooth. Re-cover the bowl and let the dough rise a second time until doubled, about 45 minutes.

Turn the dough out onto a lightly floured work surface. Divide the dough into 6 equal portions. Form each portion into a ball by rolling each small piece of dough between your cupped hand and a flour-dusted work surface. Cover the balls with a towel and let them rise on the floured surface until doubled, about 30 minutes. Meanwhile, place a baking stone in an oven and preheat to 425 degrees F.

Using your fingertips press out each ball into a disk about 2½ inches in diameter. Cover with a towel and let rise for 15 minutes.

Mist the preheated oven with a spray bottle and quickly shut the oven door. Dust a baker's peel with cornmeal. Using a soft-bristled brush, paint each disk lightly with olive oil. Using your fingertips, press "dimples" all over the surface of the disks; they should be about three quarters the depth of the thickness of the disk. Gently transfer the disks to the peel and mist the disks. With a rhythmic snap of the wrist, slide the disks onto the baking stone. Mist the oven again and bake for 5 minutes. Mist one more time and bake until the rolls are a light golden brown and have a hollow ring when tapped on the bottom, 20 to 25 minutes. Remove to wire racks, brush with olive oil, and let cool completely.

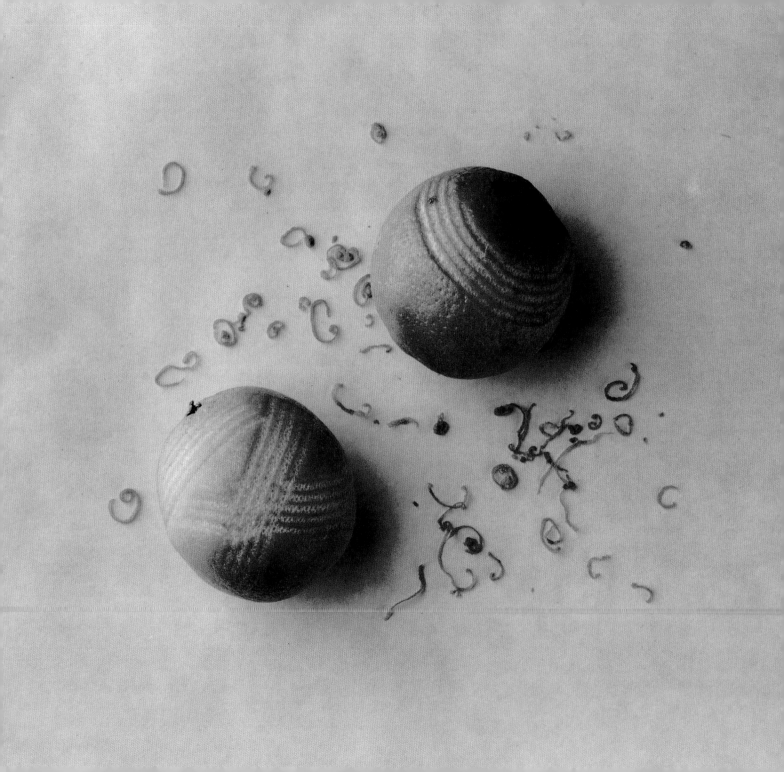

PANE DEL PESCATORE
Fisherman's Bread

◆

MAKES TWO 6-INCH LOAVES

These rich, lightly sweetened loaves are specialties of the ancient Ligurian seaport of Genoa, where fishermen have historically packed them for long sea journeys. The breads, which keep for a week or more, are dotted with raisins and with candied citrus rinds, made from the fruits of the lemon and orange groves that cover Liguria's valleys. They are an ideal late afternoon pick-me-up or a fitting finale to a Sunday brunch.

¾ cup (1½ sticks) unsalted butter, at room temperature

5 tablespoons sugar

1 whole egg

1 egg yolk

2¼ cups unbleached all-purpose flour

2 teaspoons baking powder

¾ cup golden raisins

¼ cup diced candied orange rind

¼ cup diced candied lemon rind

4 teaspoons fennel seeds

3 tablespoons milk

3 tablespoons dry Marsala

Additional flour for work surface

Additional unsalted butter for baking sheet (optional)

Preheat an oven to 350 degrees F.

In a large mixing bowl, combine the butter and sugar. Using a hand-held mixer set on medium speed, beat the ingredients until the mixture is fluffy, light, and pale in color, 5 to 7 minutes. Continuing to beat on medium speed, add the whole egg and then the egg yolk, beating well after each addition and scraping down the sides of the bowl with a rubber spatula. Set aside.

In a separate bowl stir together the flour, baking powder, raisins, candied orange and lemon rinds, and fennel seeds. Add half of the flour mixture to the butter mixture and mix on low speed until the dry ingredients are thoroughly incorporated. Beat in 2 tablespoons of the milk and the Marsala. Add the remaining flour mixture and continue to mix on low speed just until a rough, shaggy dough forms.

Turn the dough out onto a lightly floured board and knead with lightly floured hands until the dough is soft but still slightly sticky, about 2 minutes. Divide the dough into 2 equal portions. Shape each portion into a ball and then, using the palms of your hands, flatten the balls into disks about 1 inch thick.

Line a baking sheet with parchment paper or grease it with butter. Place the shaped loaves on it. With a small serrated knife, cut a simple, shallow grid pattern in the top of each loaf. Brush the tops with the remaining 1 tablespoon milk.

Bake the loaves in the preheated oven until a light golden brown and a wooden toothpick inserted in the centers comes out dry, 35 to 40 minutes. Remove to wire racks to cool completely.

◆   ◆   ◆

PIZZE

Pizzas

PASTA DI PIZZA ALLA
NAPOLETANA
Basic Pizza Dough from Naples 98

❖

SALSA PER LA PIZZA
Basic Pizza Sauce 100

❖

PIZZA MARGHERITA
Pizza with Tomatoes, Mozzarella, and Basil 102

❖

PIZZA LUGANEGA
Pizza with Sausage 103

❖

PIZZA MARINARA
Pizza with Tomato, Eggplant, and Basil 104

❖

PIZZA PUGLIESE
*Pizza with Tomato, Black Olives,
Capers, and Garlic* 105

❖

PIZZA QUATTRO STAGIONI
*Pizza with Artichokes, Tomatoes,
Mushrooms, and Ham* 107

❖

CALZONE DEL SALUMIERE
*Folded Pizza Filled with Pancetta,
Sausage, and Cheeses* 108

❖

CALZONE MEZZADRO
*Folded Pizza Filled with Potatoes,
Eggs, and Sausage* 110

❖

FOCACCIA AL GORGONZOLA,
BASILICO, E PINOLI
*Focaccia Filled with Gorgonzola,
Basil, and Pine Nuts* 111

The contemporary pizza comes from a long line of Italian flat breads. Both Virgil and Horace wrote of rustic dough circles baked on stone hearths, but it was not until two millennia later that what we now know as pizza was born.

Tomatoes are the reason why: Almost everyone, Italian and non-Italian alike, thinks of tomato sauce when they think of pizza. And although the *pomodoro* had arrived in Europe by the sixteenth century, it took a full century and a half for it to be accepted as a suitable topping for flat breads — or, for that matter, anything else.

I made few pizzas when I worked in Italy. The tradition was born in Naples and even by the late sixties there was only a handful of pizzerias in the north where I lived.

Shortly after I came to San Francisco in 1979, I was put in charge of designing a menu for a sleek, new Italian restaurant. Authentic pizzas were just coming into vogue then, so I had a wood-burning oven installed. On the day I was to test the oven, the restaurant was still only half-finished and filled with carpenters and sawhorses. That meant I had to climb a tall ladder and crawl along the scaffolding to transport my assembled *pizza Margherita* from the kitchen to the fired-up *forno.* But the pizza turned out beautifully, and I considered it heaven-sent because, after all, it came more or less from the ceiling.

The experience made me forever superstitious when it comes to pizza making. I never open a new Il Fornaio restaurant without first christening the *forno* with a *pizza Margherita.* Neapolitan *pizzaioli* are as superstitious as I am. It is common to see figures of Santa Antonio Abate, the patron saint of bakers, placed in niches over their ovens.

PASTA DI PIZZA ALLA NAPOLETANA
Basic Pizza Dough from Naples

◆

MAKES 8 OUNCES DOUGH, ENOUGH FOR ONE 12-INCH PIZZA CRUST

This dough comes together with little trouble; do not overwork it or you will end up with a tough crust. Once you have shaped the crust, slip it onto a cornmeal-dusted baker's peel and then add the toppings. As you layer the ingredients on the dough, grasp a corner of the crust every now and again and shake the round gently to be certain that it is not sticking to the peel, or loosen the crust by shaking the peel handle. If you have neither a peel nor a baking stone, a baking sheet or a pizza pan dusted with cornmeal will work, too.

A twelve-inch pizza serves four as a first course or two as a main course. The dough can also be divided in half and formed into individual pizzas, or pizzette.

Mound the flour on a work surface. Form a well in the center and add the olive oil to the well.

In a small bowl dissolve the yeast in the warm water. Set it aside until it is creamy, about 15 minutes.

When the yeast mixture is ready, add the salt to the well along with half of the yeast mixture. Working from the center outward, with one hand gradually pull the sides of the well into the center until all of the flour is incorporated. The mixture will be very sticky.

Continue to mix the dough with both hands while adding the remaining yeast mixture in small increments. When all of the yeast mixture has been added and the ingredients are well blended, knead the dough until it is elastic, light, and no longer sticky, adding small pinches of flour only if necessary to reduce the stickiness. Do not add too much additional flour or the dough will be too dry. The kneading will take about 20 minutes, with some 1- to 2-minute rest periods along the way. Shape the dough into a ball.

Dust a large bowl with flour and place the dough in the bowl. Cover the bowl with a towel and let rise at room temperature until doubled, about 1½ hours.

Punch down the dough by pressing out most of the air with your fingertips. Shape into a ball once again, re-cover the bowl and let the dough rise for a second time until doubled, about 30 minutes.

To shape the pizza crust, invert the dough onto a lightly floured work surface and flatten it into a disk about 4 inches in diameter and 1 inch thick. Working from the center of the disk outward, press the dough out with the heels of your hands, keeping the edges thicker than the center. If the dough becomes sticky as you work with it, sprinkle a little flour over the dough and on the work surface. When the dough is about ½ inch thick at the center, begin to stretch the dough by placing one hand on the center of the round, grasping an edge of the round with the other hand, and pulling gently. Work your way around the edge until you have an even round about 12 inches in diameter and 1/16 inch thick. The edges of the round should be slightly thicker than the center and turned up and pinched lightly to form a rim.

Transfer the round to a cornmeal-dusted baker's peel, top the crust, and bake as directed in individual pizza recipes.

1 cup unbleached all-purpose flour

2 teaspoons extra-virgin olive oil

¾ teaspoon active dry yeast

⅓ cup plus 1 tablespoon warm water (105 degrees F)

½ teaspoon salt

Additional flour for work surface and bowl

Medium-grind yellow cornmeal for baker's peel

SALSA PER LA PIZZA
Basic Pizza Sauce

◆

The best pizzas have only a light coating of sauce, so as not to mask the flavors of the dough and toppings. Select the sweetest, vine-ripened plum pomodori for the brightest, fullest taste.

4 ounces vine-ripened plum tomatoes (2 or 3)

2 fresh basil leaves

¼ teaspoon salt

Pinch of freshly ground black pepper

½ tablespoon extra-virgin olive oil

1 heaping tablespoon tomato purée

1 clove garlic

Trim off the stem and base ends of the tomatoes, but do not peel. Place the tomatoes in a food processor fitted with a metal blade. Add the basil leaves and purée until smooth. Alternatively, chop the basil leaves and pass them and the tomatoes through a food mill. Pour the mixture into a bowl and add the salt, pepper, oil, and tomato purée.

Peel the garlic clove but leave it whole. Place it on a firm surface and, using the heel of your hand, smash it to release its flavor. Add the garlic to the tomato mixture and stir until the ingredients are thoroughly combined. Let stand for a while to allow the flavors to blend. If desired, discard the garlic clove before using the sauce.

◆　　◆　　◆

PIZZA MARGHERITA
Pizza with Tomatoes, Mozzarella, and Basil

◆

MAKES ONE 12-INCH PIZZA; SERVES 2 TO 4

1 recipe Pasta di Pizza alla Napoletana dough (page 98)

1 recipe Salsa per la Pizza (page 100)

Medium-grind yellow cornmeal for baker's peel

1 tablespoon freshly grated Parmesan cheese

3½ ounces mozzarella cheese, shredded

2 fresh basil leaves, cut into thin strips

½ tablespoon extra-virgin olive oil

Pinch of chopped fresh oregano

Additional olive oil for crust

This unpretentious pizza has royal origins. It takes its name from Queen Margherita of Savoy, who first sampled it one evening in 1889, at a party given in her honor at the Campodimonte Palace in Naples. The queen, who had never before tasted southern Italy's famous savory pie, was served a variety of pizzas that night, baked by the city's most famous pizzaiolo, Don Raffaele Esposito. She is reported to have favored this one above all. Local pundits insisted her preference was due to the pie's red, green, and white ingredients, which reminded the patriotic monarch of her beloved Italy's flag.

Prepare the pizza dough and pizza sauce.

Place a baking stone in an oven and preheat to 475 degrees F. Shape the dough into a large round as directed in the dough recipe. Dust a baker's peel with cornmeal and slip the pizza crust onto the peel. Spoon the sauce onto the round and, using the back of the spoon, spread the sauce evenly over the crust. Sprinkle the Parmesan cheese over the top, and then scatter the mozzarella cheese over the sauce, followed by the basil. Drizzle the olive oil evenly over the top and sprinkle with the oregano.

With a rhythmic snap of the wrist, slide the pizza onto the stone and bake until the cheese is melted and the crust is golden brown and puffy, 12 to 15 minutes. Remove from the oven, brush the edges of the crust with olive oil, cut into wedges, and serve immediately.

◆ ◆ ◆

PIZZA LUGANEGA

Pizza with Sausage

◆

Luganega *is a mildly seasoned, thin pork sausage. It takes its name from ancient Lucania, the region of the southern Italian boot now known as Basilicata. So adept were the Lucanians in the art of cured meats that their name became synonymous with sausage — and even today, variations on the word* luganega *mean "sausage" in the languages of Spain, Greece, the Philippines, and parts of the Middle East.*

Prepare the pizza dough and pizza sauce.

While the dough is rising, place a baking stone in an oven and preheat to 450 degrees F. Cut the pepper in half lengthwise and remove and discard the seeds and ribs. Arrange the pepper halves, skin side up, in a small, shallow baking pan and brush with olive oil. Place in the oven and roast until the skin is blackened, about 20 minutes. The skin is sufficiently blackened when about 60 percent of the surface has darkened and blistered. Remove from the oven, transfer to a bowl, and increase the oven heat to 475 degrees F. Cover the bowl tightly and let stand for 20 minutes. Now, using your fingertips, peel the skin from the pepper. Slice the pepper lengthwise into ½-inch-wide strips. Set aside.

Shape the dough into a large round as directed in the dough recipe. Dust a baker's peel with cornmeal and slip the pizza crust onto the peel. Spoon the sauce onto the round and, using the back of the spoon, spread it evenly over the crust. Sprinkle the Parmesan cheese over the top, and then scatter the mozzarella cheese over the sauce, followed by the basil. Strew the sausage chunks over the cheese and arrange the pepper strips evenly across the top. Drizzle the olive oil evenly over the top and sprinkle with the oregano.

With a rhythmic snap of the wrist, slide the pizza onto the stone and bake until the cheese is melted and the crust is golden brown and puffy, 12 to 15 minutes. Remove from the oven, brush the edges of the crust with olive oil, cut into wedges, and serve immediately.

◆ ◆ ◆

1 recipe Pasta di Pizza alla Napoletana dough (page 98)

1 cup Salsa per la Pizza (page 100)

1 small red sweet pepper (about 3 ounces)

Extra-virgin olive oil for sweet pepper

Medium-grind yellow cornmeal for baker's peel

1 tablespoon freshly grated Parmesan cheese

3½ ounces mozzarella cheese, shredded

2 fresh basil leaves, cut into thin strips

1 sweet Italian sausage (about 2½ ounces), casing removed and meat broken into small chunks

½ tablespoon extra-virgin olive oil

Pinch of chopped fresh oregano

Additional olive oil for crust

PIZZA MARINARA
Pizza with Tomato, Eggplant, and Basil

◆

MAKES ONE 12-INCH PIZZA; SERVES 2 TO 4

1 recipe Pasta di Pizza alla Napoletana dough (page 98)

1 recipe Salsa per la Pizza (page 100)

1 slender Asian eggplant (about 4 ounces)

Salt

1½ tablespoons extra-virgin olive oil

1 large clove garlic, thinly sliced lengthwise

Medium-grind yellow cornmeal for baker's peel

1 tablespoon freshly grated Parmesan cheese

2 plum tomatoes or 1 large tomato (about 3 ounces), thinly sliced

2 thin slices red onion, halved and separated into half rings

2 fresh basil leaves, cut into thin strips

Pinch of minced fresh oregano

Additional olive oil for crust

This is technically a poor person's pizza — a marinara is the workaday uniform worn by ordinary seamen on Italian sailing ships. But it is rich with the simple pleasures of the peasant garden that no expense can equal: fresh tomatoes, eggplant, and basil.

Prepare the pizza dough and pizza sauce.

Place a baking stone in an oven and preheat to 475 degrees F. Trim off and discard the ends of the eggplant and slice very thinly lengthwise. Arrange the slices in a fan shape on a dish and sprinkle a little salt over each slice. Let stand for 15 minutes. Shake off the excess salt and arrange the eggplant slices in a single layer in a shallow baking pan. Brush the slices evenly with 1 tablespoon of the oil and place in the oven until just tender when pierced, about 10 minutes. Remove from the oven and set aside.

Meanwhile, bring a small amount of water to a boil. Place the garlic in a cup, pour the boiling water over the top, and let stand for 4 to 5 minutes. Drain, transfer the garlic slices to a paper towel, and pat dry.

Shape the dough into a large round as directed in the dough recipe. Dust a baker's peel with cornmeal and slip the pizza crust onto the peel. Spoon the sauce onto the round and, using the back of the spoon, spread it evenly over the crust. Sprinkle the Parmesan cheese over the top. Arrange the tomato slices over the sauce, followed by the eggplant slices. Scatter the garlic, onion, and basil over the surface and then drizzle with the remaining ½ tablespoon olive oil. Top with the oregano and a healthy pinch of salt.

With a rhythmic snap of the wrist, slide the pizza onto the stone and bake until the cheese is melted and the crust is golden brown and puffy, 12 to 15 minutes. Remove from the oven, brush the edges of the crust with olive oil, cut into wedges, and serve immediately.

PIZZA PUGLIESE

Pizza with Tomato, Black Olives, Capers, and Garlic

◆

MAKES ONE 12-INCH PIZZA; SERVES 2 TO 4

The southern Italian region of Apulia is a sunny cornucopia of vineyards and farms. It is especially noted for its vegetable dishes, including the celebrated orecchiette alla barese, *pasta in the shape of little ears tossed with olive oil and broccoli raab. This vegetarian pizza features one of Apulia's agricultural debts to Greece, which lies just across the Adriatic: the savory black olive.*

Prepare the pizza dough and pizza sauce.

Place a baking stone in an oven and preheat to 475 degrees F. Meanwhile, bring a small amount of water to a boil. Place the garlic in a cup, pour the boiling water over the top, and let stand for 4 to 5 minutes. Drain, transfer the garlic slices to a paper towel, and pat dry. Place the olives, one by one, on a firm surface and hit them decisively with the heel of your hand to release the pit and divide the olive in half. Rinse the capers under cool water and pat dry with a paper towel.

Shape the dough into a large round as directed in the dough recipe. Dust a baker's peel with cornmeal and slip the pizza crust onto the peel. Spoon the sauce onto the round and, using the back of the spoon, spread it evenly over the crust. Sprinkle the Parmesan cheese evenly over the top. Scatter the mozzarella cheese over the sauce, and then strew over the olives, capers, and garlic. Drizzle the olive oil evenly over the top and sprinkle with the pepper flakes and oregano.

With a rhythmic snap of the wrist, slide the pizza onto the stone and bake until the cheese is melted and the crust is golden brown and puffy, 12 to 15 minutes. Remove from the oven, brush the edges of the crust with olive oil, cut into wedges, and serve immediately.

1 recipe Pasta di Pizza alla Napoletana *dough (page 98)*

1 recipe Salsa per la Pizza *(page 100)*

2 extra-large cloves garlic, thinly sliced crosswise

2 ounces Gaeta or Kalamata olives (20 to 25)

1 tablespoon capers

Medium-grind yellow cornmeal for baker's peel

1 tablespoon freshly grated Parmesan cheese

3½ ounces mozzarella cheese, shredded

½ tablespoon extra-virgin olive oil

¼ teaspoon red pepper flakes

Pinch of chopped fresh oregano

Additional olive oil for crust

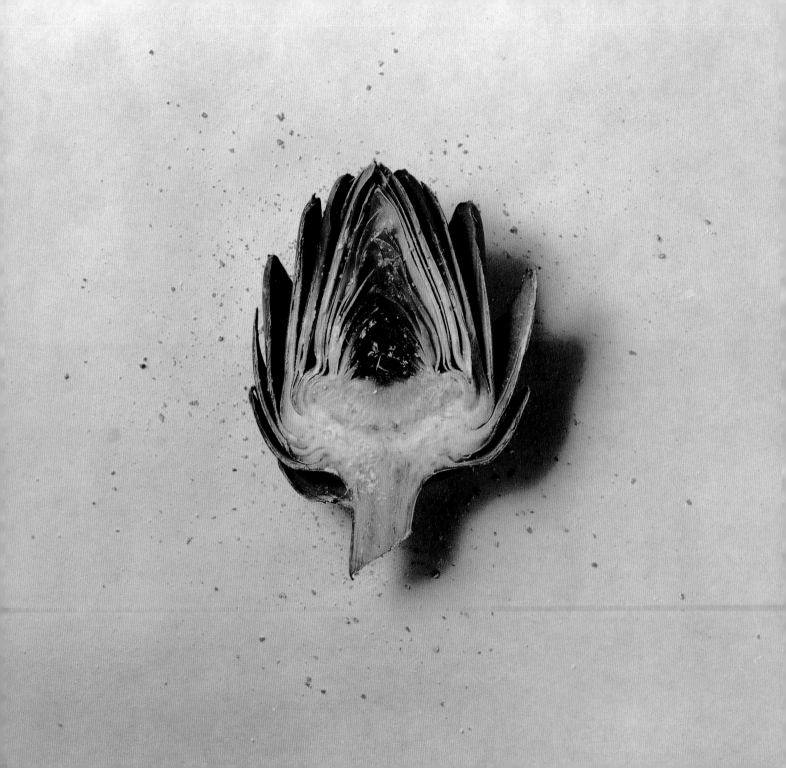

PIZZA QUATTRO STAGIONI
Pizza with Artichokes, Tomatoes, Mushrooms, and Ham

◆

MAKES ONE 12-INCH PIZZA; SERVES 2 TO 4

Italians are divided on whether the pizza Margherita or the pizza quattro stagioni is the country's most popular pie. I refuse to take sides in the debate. But there is no question that the quattro stagioni is one of Italy's most richly embellished pizzas, with each ingredient a seasonal salute: spring artichokes, summer tomatoes, fall mushrooms, and winter ham.

Prepare the pizza dough and pizza sauce.

Place a baking stone in an oven and preheat to 475 degrees F. Shape the dough into a large round as directed in the dough recipe. Dust a baker's peel with cornmeal and slip the pizza crust onto the peel. Spoon the sauce onto the round and, using the back of the spoon, spread it evenly over the crust. Sprinkle the Parmesan cheese evenly over the top and scatter the mozzarella cheese over the sauce.

Visually divide the pizza into four quarters. Starting in the upper left-hand corner, arrange the artichokes in the quarter. Proceeding clock-wise, arrange the mushrooms in the next quarter, the tomatoes in the next, and, lastly, the ham slices in the lower left-hand quarter. Strew the basil evenly over the four quarters. Sprinkle the oregano over the artichokes and ham and the salt over the tomatoes and mushrooms. Drizzle the olive oil evenly over the top.

With a rhythmic snap of the wrist, slide the pizza onto the stone and bake until the cheese is melted and the crust is golden brown and puffy, 12 to 15 minutes. Remove from the oven, brush the edges of the crust with olive oil, cut into wedges, and serve immediately.

◆ ◆ ◆

1 recipe Pasta di Pizza alla Napoletana dough (page 98)

1 recipe Salsa per la Pizza (page 100)

Medium-grind yellow cornmeal for baker's peel

1 tablespoon freshly grated Parmesan cheese

3½ ounces mozzarella cheese, shredded

3 marinated whole artichoke hearts (about 3 ounces), drained and cut into quarters lengthwise

3 or 4 fresh cultivated mushrooms (about 2 ounces), thinly sliced and slices halved crosswise

1 vine-ripened plum tomato or small round tomato (about 2 ounces), thinly sliced

1 ounce thinly sliced cooked ham

3 fresh basil leaves, cut into thin strips

Pinch of chopped fresh oregano

Pinch of salt

½ tablespoon extra-virgin olive oil

Additional olive oil for crust

The mid-eighteenth century saw the publication of Usi e costumi di Napoli, a detailed description of everyday Neapolitan life. In it appears a list of the most common pizzas of the time, among which were pies with oil and garlic and with lard, cheese, and basil. A topping of mozzarella and tomato was dismissed as being a particularly esoteric combination.

Pizza toppings have continued to evolve since those early days, including many without tomatoes. Potatoes with anchovies and scamorza, Gorgonzola with walnuts and garlic, or spinach with provolone are just a few of the possibilities. Experiment with combinations, but remember to limit the ingredients so their individual flavors come through.

CALZONE DEL SALUMIERE
Folded Pizza Filled with Pancetta, Sausage, and Cheeses

◆

MAKES 1 LARGE FOLDED PIZZA; SERVES 2 TO 4

Calzone *means "pant leg." It is likely the Italians christened this savory package a* calzone *because of its resemblance to the billowy trouser legs favored by Neapolitan men in the eighteenth and nineteenth centuries when the folded pizza was just getting its start. Whatever its etymology, the* calzone *is clearly a close kin of the legendary pie, although it does depart from its better-known relative on one important issue: Whereas southern Italians believe pizza tastes best when eaten while grasped in the hand, a* calzone *calls for the more formal trappings of a plate and a knife and fork. It also promises to carry a more plentiful filling than the pizza, which means it is particularly favored by anyone with* un appetito grande.

A salumiere *is a delicatessen worker, someone who understands the complex world of Italian* salumi *("cold cuts"), fresh sausages, and cheeses. This plump turnover, filled with a quintet of meats and cheeses, is my homage to that estimable profession.*

◆　　◆　　◆

Prepare the pizza dough.

While the dough is rising, place a baking stone in an oven and preheat to 450 degrees F. Cut the pepper in half lengthwise and remove and discard the seeds and ribs. Arrange the pepper halves, skin side up, in a small, shallow baking pan and brush with olive oil. Place in the oven and roast until the skin is blackened, about 20 minutes. The skin is sufficiently blackened when about 60 percent of the surface has darkened and blistered. Remove from the oven, transfer to a bowl, and increase the oven temperature to 475 degrees F. Cover the bowl tightly and let stand for 20 minutes. Now, using your fingertips, peel the skin from the pepper. Slice the pepper lengthwise into ½-inch-wide strips. Set aside.

Meanwhile, preheat a broiler. Place the sausage and *pancetta* in a shallow flameproof pan and slip under the broiler. Broil until both meats are cooked, 3 to 4 minutes. Remove from the oven, drain off the accumulated fat, and set aside.

Bring a small amount of water to a boil. Place the garlic in a cup, pour the boiling water over the top, and let stand for 4 to 5 minutes. Drain, transfer the garlic slices to a paper towel, and pat dry.

Shred 2 ounces of the mozzarella and place in a bowl. Cut the remaining 1 ounce of mozzarella into 2 long, thin slices and set aside. Add the garlic, ricotta cheese, goat cheese, salt, black pepper, and thyme to the bowl holding the shredded mozzarella and stir until well combined. Set aside.

On a lightly floured work surface and using a rolling pin, roll out the dough into an oval about 16 inches long, 13 inches wide at its broadest point, and ¹⁄₁₆ inch thick. Facing a long side of the oval, position the 2 mozzarella slices side-by-side and overlapping slightly on the center of the oval half nearest you. Strew the ricotta mixture evenly over the mozzarella. Arrange the sausage and *pancetta* over the cheeses and then scatter the roasted pepper strips and onion slices over the top.

Using a soft-bristled brush, paint the edges of the oval with the egg. Pick up the long oval edge farthest from you and fold it toward you, enclosing the filling completely. Pinch the top and bottom edges together with your fingertips. Trim away excess dough to form a uniform half-moon shape and press the edges with the tines of a fork to seal securely.

Dust a baker's peel with cornmeal and slip the *calzone* onto the peel. Poke 3 or 4 small holes in the top of the *calzone*. Brush with olive oil and sprinkle with the Parmesan cheese. With a rhythmic snap of the wrist, slide the *calzone* onto the stone and bake until the crust is golden brown, 12 to 15 minutes. Remove from the oven, cut crosswise, and serve immediately.

1 recipe Pasta di Pizza alla Napoletana *dough (page 98)*

1 small red sweet pepper (about 3 ounces)

Extra-virgin olive oil for sweet pepper

1 small or ½ medium-sized sweet Italian sausage (about 1½ ounces), casing removed and meat broken into small chunks

1½ ounces thinly sliced pancetta, *cut into long, ¼-inch-wide strips*

1 large clove garlic, thinly sliced lengthwise

3 ounces mozzarella cheese

2 ounces ricotta cheese

1½ ounces soft goat cheese

¼ teaspoon salt

⅛ teaspoon freshly ground black pepper

½ teaspoon chopped fresh thyme leaves

Unbleached all-purpose flour for work surface

2 thin slices red onion, separated into rings

1 egg, beaten

Medium-grind yellow cornmeal for baker's peel

Additional olive oil for top crust

½ tablespoon freshly grated Parmesan cheese

CALZONE MEZZADRO
Folded Pizza Filled with Potatoes, Eggs, and Sausage

◆

The calzone, which is nothing more than a pizza that is stuffed and folded into a half-moon, traditionally encloses a standard pizza filling. But here I've broken with custom and slipped an all-American breakfast into the venerable Neapolitan package.

1 recipe Pasta di Pizza
    alla Napoletana
    dough (page 98)

1 tablespoon extra-
    virgin olive oil

1 tablespoon vegetable oil

3 thin slices red onion,
    separated into rings

1 red potato (about 2½
    ounces), unpeeled,
    very thinly sliced
    crosswise

1 sweet Italian sausage
    (about 2 ounces),
    casing removed and
    meat broken into
    small chunks

4 eggs

4 tablespoons (½ stick)
    unsalted butter

3 sprigs fresh sage

Unbleached all-purpose
    flour for work
    surface

Medium-grind yellow
    cornmeal for baker's
    peel

1 teaspoon freshly grated
    Parmesan cheese

Prepare the pizza dough.

Place a baking stone in an oven and preheat to 475 degrees F. In an ovenproof skillet over medium heat, warm the olive oil and vegetable oil. Add the onion slices, sauté briefly, and then scatter the potato slices over the top. Cook just until the onion begins to brown, 3 to 4 minutes. Remove the skillet from the heat, place the sausage in it, and transfer the skillet to the pre-heated oven. Bake until the sausage is cooked, about 15 minutes; do not brown too much.

Using a slotted utensil, remove the onion mix-ture and set aside. Break 3 of the eggs into a small bowl and beat until blended. Return the skillet to medium heat to warm the pan juices. When hot, pour in the eggs and scramble gently until cooked but still slightly "wet"; they will cook fully inside the *calzone*. Set the eggs aside to cool.

In a small saucepan over medium heat, melt the butter with the sage. Continue to heat until the butter begins to turn a hazelnut color, then remove from the heat and set aside.

On a lightly floured work surface and using a rolling pin, roll out the dough into an oval about 16 inches long, 13 inches wide at its broadest point, and ⅟16 inch thick. Facing a long side of the oval, arrange the onion mixture in the center of the oval half nearest you. Top with the eggs.

In a small bowl lightly beat the remaining egg. Using a soft-bristled brush, paint the edges of the oval with the egg. Pick up the long oval edge farthest from you and fold it toward you, enclosing the filling completely. Pinch the top and bottom edges together with your fingertips. Trim away excess dough to form a uniform half-moon shape and press the edges with the tines of a fork to seal securely.

Dust a baker's peel with cornmeal and slip the *calzone* onto the peel. Poke 3 or 4 small holes in the top of the *calzone*. Brush with the reserved sage butter, place the sage sprigs on top, and sprinkle with the Parmesan cheese. With a rhyth-mic snap of the wrist, slide the *calzone* onto the stone and bake until the crust is golden brown, 12 to 15 minutes. Remove from the oven, cut crosswise, and serve immediately.

FOCACCIA AL GORGONZOLA, BASILICO, E PINOLI

Focaccia Filled with Gorgonzola, Basil, and Pine Nuts

◆

In *the picturesque Ligurian fishermen's town of Recco,* focaccia al formaggio — *soft, runny* stracchino *cheese sealed in a crisp crust — is a trademark of the local bakers. Despite its name, the resolutely modest dish is made with a thin, easily stretched pizza-type dough and not a thicker* focaccia *dough. This is my own version of that seaside specialty, which mixes two cheeses and adds pine nuts and basil.*

Prepare the pizza dough.

Place a baking stone in an oven and preheat to 500 degrees F. On a lightly floured work surface and using a rolling pin, roll out the dough into a rectangle about 16 inches long, 10 inches wide, and 1/16 inch thick. Facing a long side of the rectangle, position the 2 mozzarella slices, side-by-side and slightly overlapping, in the center of the half of the rectangle nearest you. Scatter the Gorgonzola evenly over the mozzarella and then strew about half of the onion over the top. Sprinkle evenly with the basil and pine nuts.

Using a soft-bristled brush, paint the edges of the rectangle with the egg. Pick up the long rectangle edge farthest from you and fold it toward you, enclosing the filling completely.

Pinch the top and bottom edges together with your fingertips. Trim away excess dough to form clean, straight edges and press with the tines of a fork to seal securely.

Dust a baker's peel with cornmeal and slip the filled *focaccia* onto the peel. Poke 3 or 4 small holes in the top and then arrange the remaining onion on top. With a rhythmic snap of the wrist, slide the *focaccia* onto the stone and bake until the crust is golden, 12 to 15 minutes. You may need to turn the *focaccia* over after 8 minutes to ensure even baking. Remove from the oven, then drizzle with olive oil and sprinkle with the Parmesan cheese. Cut into 6 or 8 squares and serve immediately.

1 recipe Pasta di Pizza alla Napoletana dough (page 98)

Unbleached all-purpose flour for work surface

2½ ounces mozzarella cheese, cut into 2 long, thin slices

2½ ounces Gorgonzola cheese, crumbled

3 thin slices red onion, quartered and separated into quarter rings

4 or 5 fresh basil leaves, finely chopped

1 tablespoon pine nuts, lightly toasted

1 egg, lightly beaten

Medium-grind yellow cornmeal for baker's peel

Extra-virgin olive oil for top crust

½ tablespoon freshly grated Parmesan cheese

◆ ◆ ◆

Le Ricette del Giorno Dopo

Recipes Using Leftover Breads

BRUSCHETTA
*Toasted Bread with Garlic, Olive
Oil, and Tomatoes* 116

❖

CROSTINI
*Toasted Bread with
Assorted Toppings* 117

❖

CROSTINI ALL'AGIO
Garlic Croutons 119

❖

RISCALDATA
Baked Vegetable Soup with Bread 121

❖

CARCIOFI RIPIENI
*Artichokes Stuffed with
Bread, Artichoke Hearts, Lemon,
and Capers* 122

❖

PANZANELLA
Bread, Tomato, and Basil Salad 123

❖

PANE GRATTUGGIATO
Bread Crumbs 123

❖

RIBOLLITA
*Tuscan Vegetable Soup
with Bread* 125

❖

PAPPA AL POMODORO
*Tuscan Bread Soup with Tomato,
Herbs, and Olive Oil* 127

❖

BUDINO DI PANE
*Bread Pudding with
Raisins and Rum* 128

When I was growing up, my mother worked as a chef at nearby Lake Garda in the summer and in our town the rest of the year. In the 1970s, she had her own restaurant on the lake, the Albergo Ristorante Stella. She was known for her *casunsei*, our dialect for ravioli stuffed with sausage, bread crumbs, and Parmesan. I learned how to make many dishes from her — *ossobuco*, *tortellini* filled with chard, *risotto* with *porcini*. From watching her, I knew I wanted to cook, too.

My father's cousins owned the best restaurant in Carpenedolo, the Albergo Ristorante Bolzoni. It was so popular, traveling businesspeople regularly routed themselves through town at midday just so they could eat lunch there. In the summer of my fourteenth year, my grandfather arranged a job for me at Bolzoni. In those days, most restaurant chefs were women and it was difficult for a young man to land a position in a kitchen. The chef at Bolzoni did not like the idea of having me in her kitchen, so most of the time I was put out front to serve drinks. But I stole glances into the *cucina* and soon I understood why Italians are among the world's thriftiest chefs.

At the bakery it was my job to put unsold loaves of bread atop the oven, so that they would dry for crushing into crumbs. At Bolzoni, I saw how leftover bread was used in soups, to stuff vegetables and poultry, and in pasta fillings. Bread was never wasted; it was simply transformed into another wonderful dish.

The menus at the Il Fornaio restaurants include many dishes that contain leftover bread, from the popular Roman *bruschetta* to the rustic Tuscan soup *ribollita*. They are simple yet satisfying plates that reflect the Italians' love of bread and respect for frugality.

BRUSCHETTA
Toasted Bread with Garlic, Olive Oil, and Tomatoes

SERVES 4

8 cups water

2 pounds vine-ripened plum tomatoes (about 16)

12 to 14 fresh basil leaves, cut into thin, long strips

¼ cup plus 4 teaspoons extra-virgin olive oil

Salt and freshly ground black pepper

8 slices Filone (page 48), each about 1 inch thick

1 extra-large clove garlic

For the simplest bruschetta, a Roman specialty that also has the ribald nickname schiena d'asino — *"the back of a jackass"* — hot toasted bread slices are rubbed with garlic cloves and then drizzled with fruity olive oil. This summertime version, more properly called bruschetta al pomodoro, *is a respectable finish for a* filone *that is beginning to show its age.*

Any cigar-shaped loaf with a light, crisp crust and soft interior can be used in place of the filone.

Preheat a broiler.

In a large saucepan bring the water to a boil. Trim the stem end off of each tomato and then cut a shallow cross in the bottom. Drop the tomatoes in the boiling water and boil just until the skins loosen, about 1 minute. Drain the tomatoes, then peel off and discard the tomato skins. (If the tomatoes are too hot to hold, use a towel to secure them with one hand and peel with the other.) Cut each tomato into quarters lengthwise and then in half crosswise. Place in a bowl, add the basil, and toss well. Add the ¼ cup olive oil and salt and pepper to taste. Mix well and set aside.

Brush the bread slices on one side only with the 4 teaspoons olive oil. Arrange on a baking sheet, oiled sides up. Slip under the preheated broiler and broil until the edges begin to brown, 1 to 1½ minutes. Flip each slice and broil until the second side begins to brown, 30 seconds to 1 minute. Remove from the oven and place oiled sides up on a heated platter.

Cutting lengthwise, slice off about one third of the garlic clove and discard the small piece. Rub the oiled surface of each piece of toast with the cut side of the garlic clove. Rub firmly enough to impart a gentle fragrance of garlic to each piece. Spoon the tomato mixture evenly over the toasts and serve immediately.

CROSTINI

Toasted Bread with Assorted Toppings

◆

MAKES ABOUT 40 CROSTINI

Crostini originated in Tuscany, where the two preferred toppings are chicken liver and olives. Their popularity is no surprise, for the region is famous for both its world-class poultry farms and its countless olives groves. Tuscan meals commonly open with a plate of the local prosciutto and two or three crostini *smeared with a warm, delicate chicken liver spread or a tangy mixture of black and green olives.*

This recipe makes about forty crostino bases, and each of the topping recipes that follow makes enough to cover about twenty bases. If you are preparing the crostini *as a first course, a full recipe will serve eight to ten generously. They also make delicious hors d'oeuvres. Use any classic baguette in place of* sfilatino. *Spread the topping on the toasted bread just before serving.*

Preheat a broiler. Prepare any two of the toppings on pages 118 and 119 and set aside.

Cut 1 loaf *Sfilatino* (page 42) on the diagonal into about forty ⅜-inch-thick slices. Arrange the slices in a single layer on 2 baking sheets. Brush both sides of each slice with extra-virgin olive oil, using about 6 tablespoons oil in all.

One at a time, slip the baking sheets under the broiler until the bread slices brown lightly, 1 to 1½ minutes. Watch carefully, as they burn easily. Flip each slice and broil until the second side browns, 30 seconds to 1 minute. Remove from the oven and let cool.

Spread the toasts thinly with the toppings. Serve at room temperature.

ITALIAN
ARTICHOKE
ANNALS

◆

Florence-born Catherine de' Medici not only craved Tuscan-grown artichokes — especially cooked up into fritters — but, upon tying the knot with King Henri II of France, she also taught her new subjects to eat the thorny vegetable. (Because the artichoke was considered an aphrodisiac, the queen's appreciation of the carciofo prompted plenty of whispering in society circles.)

The Romans are famous for two artichoke preparations, alla giudia, or "Jewish style," cooked in a deep pool of extra-virgin olive oil, and alla romana, flavored with mint. In Sardinia, small, young artichokes are eaten raw or fried. And in Sicily, where they have been popular since the time of the Saracens, these thistles are simmered with fava beans and peas, to produce a dish called fritteda.

Olive Topping

◆

5 ounces Gaeta or other
Italian black olives
5 ounces Sicilian-style
or other Italian green
olives
4 cups water
2 cloves garlic
1 lemon
8 sprigs fresh parsley,
chopped
2 tablespoons extra-
virgin olive oil
¼ teaspoon freshly
ground black pepper

In a small saucepan combine the black and green olives, the water, and the garlic cloves. Remove the zest in a few strips from half of the lemon and add them to the pan. Bring to a boil and boil gently for 20 minutes. (This step enhances the flavor of the olives and reduces some of their saltiness.) Drain, discard the garlic and zest, and let cool.

Place the olives, one by one, on a firm work surface and firmly press on them with the heel of your hand to release the pits. Chop the olives and gather them into a mound. Cut some of the remaining zest from the lemon and chop it to measure ½ teaspoon. Add it to the mound along with the chopped parsley and mince together until well combined. Scoop up into a bowl and then stir in the olive oil and pepper.

Tomato Topping

◆

12 ounces vine-ripened
plum tomatoes (6
or 7)
8 to 10 fresh basil
leaves, finely chopped
2 tablespoons extra-
virgin olive oil
¼ teaspoon salt
¼ teaspoon freshly
ground black pepper
½ teaspoon garlic salt

For the best result, select only sweet, full-flavored tomatoes for this topping. Trim off the stem and base ends of the tomatoes, but do not peel. Chop the tomatoes finely. Scoop up the tomatoes into a bowl.

Add the basil, olive oil, salt, pepper, and garlic salt. Using a spoon stir until well mixed. Taste and adjust the seasoning with salt and pepper.

Mushroom Topping

◆

2 sprigs fresh Italian
parsley, chopped
½ clove garlic
2 tablespoons unsalted
butter
2 tablespoons extra-
virgin olive oil
7 or 8 fresh cultivated
mushrooms (about 5
ounces), quartered
2 tablespoons dry white
wine
¼ teaspoon salt
⅛ teaspoon freshly
ground black pepper

Combine the parsley and garlic on a work surface and chop together finely; set aside.

In a skillet over medium heat, melt the butter with the olive oil. Add the mushrooms and sauté for 2 minutes. Add the wine, raise the heat to high, and continue to sauté until the wine reduces slightly, about 1 minute. Lower the heat to medium-high, stir in the parsley-garlic mixture, salt, and pepper and continue to sauté until the mushrooms are tender, 2 to 3 minutes. Remove from the heat, let cool, and chop finely.

Artichoke and Roasted Pepper Topping

MAKES ABOUT 1 1/3 CUPS; ENOUGH FOR ABOUT 20 CROSTINI

Preheat an oven to 450 degrees F.

Cut the pepper in half lengthwise and remove and discard the seeds and ribs. Arrange the pepper halves, skin side up, in a small, shallow pan and brush with olive oil. Place in the oven and roast until the skin is blackened, about 20 minutes. The skin is sufficiently blackened when about 60 percent of the surface has darkened and blistered.

Remove from the oven and transfer to a bowl. Cover the bowl tightly and let stand for 20 minutes. Now, using your fingertips, peel the skin from the pepper. Chop the pepper finely.

In a small bowl combine the sweet pepper, artichokes, parsley, olive oil, vinegar, and ground pepper. Mix well.

1 sweet red pepper (about 5 ounces)

Extra-virgin olive oil for sweet pepper

5 marinated whole artichoke hearts (about 5 ounces), well drained, halved lengthwise, and finely chopped

4 sprigs fresh Italian parsley, finely chopped

2 tablespoons extra-virgin olive oil

1 teaspoon red wine vinegar

¼ teaspoon freshly ground black pepper

CROSTINI ALL'AGLIO
Garlic Croutons

MAKES ABOUT 60 CROUTONS

Preheat an oven to 450 degrees F.

Combine the garlic and parsley on a work surface and chop together finely. Scoop up into a small bowl and add the olive oil, salt, and pepper. Stir well.

Arrange the bread slices in a single layer on 2 baking sheets. Brush the tops with the oil mixture and sprinkle with the Parmesan. Place in the preheated oven and bake until the cheese melts and the bread is golden, 6 to 8 minutes. Let cool and serve with green salads or float on soups. Store in an airtight container for up to 1 week.

2 cloves garlic

8 sprigs fresh parsley, chopped

¾ cup extra-virgin olive oil

1 teaspoon salt

¼ teaspoon freshly ground black pepper

1 loaf Sfilatino (page 30) or other baguette-type loaf, cut into ¼-inch-thick slices

¼ cup freshly grated Parmesan cheese

RISCALDATA
Baked Vegetable Soup with Bread

SERVES 6

I created this recipe for Il Fornaio's Etrusca restaurant in San Francisco with the intention of calling it ribollita. But the staff told me it was unlike any ribollita they had eaten in Tuscany — "much too thick." I solved the problem by coining a new name: riscaldata, "to warm up again." The change made everyone happy and the soup has been a big hit at the restaurant ever since.

You can also bake the soup in individual oval baking dishes for easier serving.

1 recipe Ribollita (page 125)

¼ cup freshly grated Parmesan cheese

3 tablespoons extra-virgin olive oil

4 very thin slices white onion, separated into rings

Additional 2 tablespoons freshly grated Parmesan cheese for serving (optional)

Freshly ground black pepper for serving

Prepare the ribollita as directed, up through toasting the bread and rubbing it with garlic. Arrange the bread in the bottom of a single large bowl instead of individual bowls. Pour the hot soup into the bowl, trying not to disturb the bread. If the bread begins to pop up, push it down with the back of a large spoon. Add the ¼ cup Parmesan cheese and mix it in gently without dislodging the bread. Cool completely, cover, and refrigerate at least 8 hours or as long as overnight. The soup will become very thick.

Preheat an oven to 450 degrees F. Oil a large, shallow oval or oblong baking dish with 1 tablespoon of the olive oil. (The dish should measure at least 9 by 13 inches.) Using a large, shallow spoon, transfer the soup mixture to the dish, being careful to keep the bread pieces on the bottom. This will be fairly easy, as the soup will not be the least bit soupy. Smooth the surface with the back of a wooden spoon and arrange the onions slices evenly over the top.

Place in the preheated oven until the onions begin to brown, about 30 minutes. Serve on individual plates. Drizzle each serving with about 1 teaspoon of the remaining olive oil, then sprinkle with some of the remaining Parmesan cheese, if desired. Pass a pepper mill at the table.

◆   ◆   ◆

CARCIOFI RIPIENI

Artichokes Stuffed with Bread, Artichoke Hearts, Lemon, and Capers

◆

SERVES 4

1 lemon, cut in half
4 large artichokes (about
   8 ounces each)
6 cups water
2 bay leaves
2 tablespoons extra-
   virgin olive oil
½ teaspoon salt
1 sprig fresh parsley
4 to 6 black peppercorns

For the stuffing:

5 ounces Pagnotta
   (page 34), crusts
   removed, cut into
   ¼-inch cubes (about
   1½ cups)
1 tablespoon capers,
   rinsed in water and
   patted dry
2 sprigs fresh parsley,
   coarsely chopped
   (about 1 tablespoon)
1 small clove garlic,
   coarsely chopped
Zest and juice of ½
   lemon
4 marinated whole arti-
   choke hearts (about 4
   ounces), well drained
   and coarsely chopped
6 tablespoons extra-
   virgin olive oil
1 teaspoon salt
⅛ teaspoon freshly
   ground black pepper

4 teaspoons extra-virgin
   olive oil for serving
4 teaspoons finely chopped
   vine-ripened tomato
Lemon wedges for serving

Serve these deep green artichokes as an antipasto to precede a simple plate of grilled meat or a bowl of steaming hot pasta. They can be assembled several hours in advance and refrigerated until serving time. Any crusty loaf with a soft, dense interior can be substituted for the pagnotta.

Fill a large bowl with water and squeeze the juice of ½ lemon into it. Working with 1 artichoke at a time, trim off the stem even with the bottoms. Remove and discard the tough outer leaves. Using a sharp knife cut off the top one fourth of the artichoke so that no points remain on any of the leaves. As each artichoke is trimmed, drop it into the water.

When all of the artichokes have been trimmed, place them in a single layer, stem ends up and not touching, in a saucepan and pour in the water. Squeeze in the juice of the remaining lemon half, then add the bay leaves, olive oil, salt, parsley, and peppercorns. Bring to a boil, reduce the heat to a simmer, cover, and cook until the stems are tender when pierced with a fork, about 45 minutes, rotating the artichokes a half turn or so every 12 to 15 minutes to be sure they cook evenly. Be careful that they do not overcook.

While the artichokes are cooking, make the stuffing. Place the bread cubes in a mixing bowl. Combine the capers, parsley, garlic, lemon zest, and artichoke hearts on a work surface and chop together finely. Add to the bread cubes along with the olive oil, lemon juice, salt, and pepper. Stir and mash with a wooden spoon until all of the bread is well saturated. Set aside.

Remove the cooked artichokes to a plate, stem ends up, and let stand for 15 minutes to drain well. Turn the artichokes upright and pull the leaves apart gently to open up the centers slightly. Using your fingertips, gently pull out the prickly center leaves. Then, using a small spoon, scoop out the thorny chokes, removing all of the fibrous and prickly bits.

Spoon some of the stuffing into the center of each artichoke and then slip some additional stuffing between the rows of leaves. Cover and chill for 30 minutes. Just before serving drizzle 1 teaspoon olive oil over the top of each artichoke and then garnish each with 1 teaspoon of the chopped tomato. Accompany with lemon wedges.

PANZANELLA
Bread, Tomato, and Basil Salad

◆

Both the Tuscans and the Romans (and, it often seems, everyone in between) claim as their own specialty a modest salad of dry bread soaked in oil and vinegar. The Tuscans frequently refine this peasant lunch with the addition of tuna and capers.

The bread must not be so stale that it "shatters" when cut. Pane toscano (page 38) or any dense white peasant loaf may be used in place of the pagnotta.

Place the bread cubes in a clear glass salad bowl and pour the beef stock over the top. Add the tomatoes, cucumber, and leek. Toss well. Scatter the basil over the top.

In a small bowl whisk together the olive oil, vinegar, salt and pepper. Drizzle evenly over the salad and toss thoroughly. As the salad is mixed, the bread will break up and soften.

Cover and refrigerate for 30 minutes before serving.

VARIATION   Just before serving, add I can (6½ ounces) imported Italian tuna packed in olive oil, drained and flaked, and I tablespoon capers, rinsed in water and patted dry. Toss well.

8 ounces 2-day-old Pagnotta (page 34), crusts removed, cut into 1½- to 2-inch cubes (about 3 cups)

¾ cup beef stock

8 ounces vine-ripened plum tomatoes (4 or 5), sliced lengthwise into quarters

1 small cucumber (about 6 ounces), thinly sliced

1 small leek, white part only, thinly sliced

8 to 10 fresh basil leaves, chopped

¼ cup extra-virgin olive oil

¼ cup red wine vinegar

¾ teaspoon salt

Generous ¼ teaspoon freshly ground black pepper

PANE GRATTUGGIATO
Bread Crumbs

◆

Gather up chunks of leftover bread — *filone, ciabatta, sfilatino* — and spread them out in a baking pan. Slip the pan into an oven set at the lowest possible temperature for about 2 hours. The bread is then *biscottato,* or "twice-baked," and should crumble into pieces when you touch it. Let cool.

Finely grate the toasted bread on a hand grater or in a food processor, then pass it through a fine-mesh sieve. Store in a container with a tight-fitting lid for up to a few weeks.

Other Italians like to joke that the Tuscans are mangiafagioli, a race of "bean eaters." But the Tuscans themselves wear this label as a badge of honor. They have elevated the prosaic bean to a culinary art form, according it hundreds of recipes. In the elegant food shops of Siena, piles of white cannellini and rosy borlotti beans are displayed with the aesthetic finesse a jeweler reserves for his best diamonds.

Historically, even the most noble of Florentines were proud mangiafagioli. One of the leading beans of Tuscany is a native of America, the haricot, which so impressed the sixteenth century Pope Clement VII that he immediately arranged to have a shipment sent to his royal niece, Catherine de' Medici, the queen of France.

RIBOLLITA
Tuscan Vegetable Soup with Bread

◆

SERVES 6

No two pots of ribollita *are alike — each is the personal creation of its chef. I have seen some versions of this renowned Tuscan bean-and-bread soup that are so thick that they can be eaten with a fork. Others are like a light minestrone with just a bit of pane in it. For me, the best ribollita in all of Italy is served at the beautiful Ristorante da Delfina, in the town of Carmignano overlooking the Chianti valley on the hills above Florence. Carlo, the chef, makes a soup that will hold a fork upright. He also turns out a beautiful finocchiona, the region's famed fennel-seasoned sausage.*

The name ribollita means "to boil again" (from bollire, "to boil") and, according to one story, originated with the Tuscan custom of "boiling" leftovers from the big Sunday meal — meat and vegetables — with some beans for Monday's dinner. This soup belongs to a large family of Italian zuppe that taste best when reheated, and it is a filling meal when accompanied with an insalata verde and a robust red wine.

Although I have suggested using pagnotta here, you may want to use the more traditional pane toscano (page 38) or any other large crusty loaf with a soft, white center.

2¾ cups (18 ounces) dried borlotti or cranberry beans (see Note)

4 quarts water

1½ teaspoons salt

4 cloves garlic

5 tablespoons extra-virgin olive oil

1 large white onion (about 8 ounces), finely chopped

1 large carrot, peeled and cut into ¼-inch dice

2 stalks celery, trimmed and cut into ¼-inch dice

1 leek, white and tender green portion, cut into ¼-inch dice

1 medium-large tomato (about 6 ounces), cut into ¼-inch dice

7 cups beef stock

1 sprig fresh rosemary, or 1 teaspoon dried rosemary

2 or 3 sprigs fresh thyme, or 1 teaspoon dried thyme

½ head green cabbage (about 12 ounces), cut into 1-inch chunks

6 slices Pagnotta (page 34), each about 1 inch thick

6 tablespoons freshly grated Parmesan cheese

In a large saucepan, place the beans, add cold water to cover by about 1 inch, and soak at least 8 hours or overnight. Drain. Add the 4 quarts water and bring to a boil. Add 1 teaspoon of the salt and boil gently, with lid slightly ajar, for 1 hour. Drain and set aside.

Meanwhile, chop 1 of the garlic cloves. In a large, heavy-bottomed saucepan over high heat, warm 2 tablespoons of the olive oil. Add the chopped garlic and onion and sauté until the edges of the onion are slightly browned, about 5 minutes. Add the carrot, celery, leek, and tomato and sauté until the onion begins to soften and the tomato turns pale, about 5 minutes. Add the stock and the remaining ½ teaspoon salt, bring to a boil, and boil for about 30 minutes.

Using a fork finely mash one fourth of the beans and set aside with the whole beans. Using the heel of your hand, mash 2 of the remaining garlic cloves. In a small skillet over medium-low heat, warm the remaining 3 tablespoons olive oil. Add the mashed garlic, rosemary, and thyme and sauté until the garlic is brown and the herbs are crispy, about 10 minutes. Remove from the heat.

Once the soup has boiled for 30 minutes, pour the olive oil mixture through a strainer into the soup; discard the garlic and herbs. Add the whole and mashed beans and the cabbage to the soup, reduce the heat to medium, and boil gently for 30 minutes. (The mashed beans will help to thicken the soup.)

Meanwhile, preheat an oven to 450 degrees F. Prepare the bread slices. Lightly bruise the remaining garlic clove and rub it over both sides of each bread slice. Arrange the slices on a baking sheet and place on the lowest rack in the preheated oven. When the bottoms begin to toast, after 8 to 10 minutes, flip the slices over and toast an additional 2 minutes.

To serve, place a bread slice in the bottom of each individual bowl. (Depending upon the size and shape of your bowls, you may need to cut the slices so that they fit.) Ladle the soup over the bread and then sprinkle 1 tablespoon Parmesan cheese over the top of each serving.

NOTE *Borlotti* beans are oval speckled beans, usually reddish markings on a tan background. To save time, you can use 2 cans (14 ounces each) *borlotti* or cranberry beans, drained, in place of the dried beans and add them to the soup at the same point as the cooked dried beans.

◆   ◆   ◆

PAPPA AL POMODORO
Tuscan Bread Soup with Tomato, Herbs, and Olive Oil

SERVES 6

*F*lorentines are the masters of this porridgelike pappa, or "bread soup." My mother makes a similar zuppa, called panata in northern Italy, that she insists "must be soft enough to eat even if you have no teeth."

The pappa *can be cooled and eaten at room temperature or it can be reheated. Upon cooling, the soup thickens as the bread absorbs more of the liquid, which is how the Tuscans prefer it. You may, however, thin it slightly with a little chicken stock when reheating. Any crusty peasant loaf with a soft, white center can stand in for the* ciabatta.

10 cups water

2¼ pounds vine-ripened plum tomatoes (about 20; see Note)

12 ounces Ciabatta (page 37), cut into 1-inch-thick slices

9 cups chicken stock

3 large sprigs fresh basil

¼ cup extra-virgin olive oil

3 cloves garlic, finely chopped (see Note)

½ teaspoon salt

½ teaspoon freshly ground black pepper

Additional extra-virgin olive oil for serving

Preheat an oven to 450 degrees F.

In a large saucepan bring the water to a boil. Trim the stem end off of each tomato and then cut a shallow cross in the bottom. Drop the tomatoes into the boiling water and boil just until the skins loosen, about 1 minute. Drain the tomatoes, then peel off and discard the tomato skins. (If the tomatoes are too hot to hold, use a towel to secure them with one hand and peel with the other.) Set aside.

Arrange the bread slices on a baking sheet and place on the lowest rack in the preheated oven. When the bottoms begin to toast, after 8 to 10 minutes, flip the slices over and toast an additional 3 minutes. Remove from the oven and set aside.

Meanwhile, bring the chicken stock to a boil in a large, heavy-bottomed saucepan. Halve the tomatoes lengthwise and remove the seeds. On a large work surface, chop the tomatoes finely, being careful not to lose the juices. Add the

tomatoes to the boiling stock, along with the whole basil sprigs, olive oil, and garlic. Then add the toasted bread slices and stir with a wooden spoon to incorporate thoroughly. When the soup returns to a boil, reduce the heat to low, add the salt and pepper, and boil gently, uncovered, until very thick, about 1¾ hours. Stir the soup occasionally to prevent the bread from sticking.

Scoop out the basil sprigs; return any leaves still intact to the soup and discard the stems. Ladle the soup into individual bowls and drizzle with additional olive oil to taste.

N O T E   If the tomatoes are not fully ripe, add 2 tablespoons tomato purée when adding the tomatoes to the stock.

If you want a milder garlic flavor, add the garlic cloves whole, then remove and discard just before serving the soup.

BUDINO DI PANE
Bread Pudding with Raisins and Rum

◆

SERVES 6 TO 8

The Venetians prepare this custardy bread pudding, a wintertime favorite, with either brandy or — in a more recent variation — rum. It is a true regional dessert, hardly known outside of the Veneto and a few other districts of northern Italy.

8 ounces Filone (page 48), crusts removed, cut into ¾- to 1-inch cubes (about 2½ cups)

5 whole eggs

2 egg yolks

¾ cup sugar

1 tablespoon vanilla extract

3 cups milk

1 cup whipping cream

¼ cup dark rum

Pinch of freshly grated nutmeg

6 tablespoons dark raisins

6 tablespoons golden raisins

For the crema inglese:

1 cup milk

2 tablespoons sugar

¼ vanilla bean, or ½ teaspoon vanilla extract

2 egg yolks

½ tablespoon unbleached all-purpose flour

Preheat an oven to 400 degrees F.

Spread the bread cubes in a shallow oval or oblong baking dish large enough to hold the pudding that is added later. (The dish should measure about 9 by 13 inches.) Toast in the preheated oven, turning occasionally, until crisp and dry, about 5 minutes. Do not allow to brown.

Meanwhile, place the whole eggs and egg yolks in a mixing bowl and beat with a wire whisk until well blended. Add the sugar and vanilla and whisk until incorporated. Whisk in the milk, cream, rum, and nutmeg until combined.

Scatter the dark and golden raisins over the bread cubes. Then evenly pour the egg mixture over the top and let stand for 30 minutes, occasionally mashing the bread with the back of a spoon. During this time the bread will absorb much of the custard and the mixture will expand slightly. The oven should still be set at 400 degrees F.

Place the pudding on the lowest rack in the preheated oven and bake until the top is golden and fairly firm yet bounces back slightly when pressed in the center, 40 to 50 minutes.

While the pudding is baking, make the *crema inglese.* Measure 6 tablespoons of the milk into a small, heavy-bottomed saucepan and add the sugar and vanilla bean or extract. Stir to combine and place over medium heat.

Meanwhile, place the egg yolks and flour in a mixing bowl and beat together with a wire whisk. Immediately add the remaining milk (½ cup plus 2 tablespoons) to the yolks in a slow stream, whisking continuously until well incorporated.

When the milk on the stove barely begins to boil, remove from the heat. Immediately add it to the egg mixture in a slow, steady stream, whisking continuously until completely smooth. Now pour the entire mixture back into the saucepan and place over medium heat. Whisking continuously, heat until thickened and smooth, 3 to 4 minutes. When small bubbles begin to appear at the edges of the pan, remove from the heat and pour into a clean bowl. Remove and discard the vanilla bean, if used, and set aside to cool slightly.

Remove the pudding from the oven and set aside to cool slightly. The pudding will have risen a bit during baking, but will fall again as it cools. Cut into 6 to 8 servings and transfer to individual plates. Pour some warm *crema inglese* over each serving.

BISCOTTI

Cookies

very town in Italy has its traditional *biscotti* and every bakery has its specialties. At Panificio d'Alba most customers came in for our crumbly short-crust cookies and, on All Saints' Day, for the traditional flat, thin, hard *biscotti* made in the shape of a bone.

But the premier *biscotto* bakers in Carpenedolo were at the Pasticcerria Carlini, which stood next door to the town's only cinema. I would stop by there on Sunday afternoons on the way to see a cowboy and Indian movie or my favorite, a Laurel and Hardy comedy. The owner knew I was a respected apprentice baker and he would invariably try to talk me into coming to work for him. The bribe was always the same: his extraordinary cookies. The most delicate ones were baked in molds and removing these *biscotti* from the pans always resulted in broken cookies. He would gather up the pieces for me to take to the movies.

I loved my job at Panificio d'Alba, and never thought of leaving it. But I also loved those cookies, so I always visited the Pasticcerria Carlini, knowing I would walk out with the town's most envied movie snack.

Although in America the word *biscotti* is commonly used only for twice-baked Italian bar cookies, in Italy the term applies to all cookies. This chapter contains many classic *biscotti*, from the crunchy *cantucci di Prato* of Tuscany to the light, chewy pine nut–studded *pinolate*. I have also included a couple of strictly American cookies — I call them *biscotti di zucca* and *biscotti di crusca* — unknown to the Italian palate but beloved by Il Fornaio customers on this side of the Atlantic.

BISCOTTI

ANICINI

BISCOTTI DI ZUCCA

AMARETTI

GARIBALDI

BISCOTTI ALLE MANDORLE

BISCOTTI DI CRUSCA

MEINI

PINOLATE

BACI D'ALASSIO

FAGOTTINI D'ALBICOCCA

BISCOTTI DA TÈ

CANTUCCI DI PRATO

BAKING TIPS
FOR BISCOTTI

◆

*Bake cookies in the top
two thirds of the oven.
Position the oven racks
so that the oven is evenly
divided into thirds. If
you are baking more
than one sheetful of
cookies at a time,
halfway through the
baking, switch the sheets
on the racks, turning
them each 180 degrees
as you do. Your biscotti
will bake more evenly.*

*When making cookies
that are cut out of a
dough sheet, limit the
number of times you
reroll the dough. Cut out
the cookie shapes as close
together as possible, so
that only a few dough
scraps remain to be
gathered and rolled
again. Rerolling the
dough more than once
will result in "tough
cookies."*

CANTUCCI DI PRATO

Almond Cookies from Prato

◆

MAKES ABOUT 8 DOZEN SMALL COOKIES

These hard, crunchy bars are more accurately called biscotti di Prato. *True* cantucci, which means "corners" and probably refers to the angular shape of the cookies, are made from bread dough, olive oil, aniseed, and sugar. But the wrong name has stuck here and elsewhere, and whether you call them cantucci or biscotti di Prato, they are best dipped in a glass of Vin Santo or Elba's celebrated Morellino wine before eating. The addition of hazelnuts to these Prato cookies is a custom borrowed from nearby Pistoia.

Prato, which lies about a dozen miles from Florence and has stood in its shadow for a millenium, is known not only for these biscotti but also (and more importantly) for its textiles, the manufacture of which was well established by the twelfth century.

◆ ◆ ◆

Preheat an oven to 350 degrees F.

Spread the hazelnuts in a single layer in a shallow pan and place them in the preheated oven, turning every now and again, until lightly toasted and the skins begin to blister, 15 to 18 minutes. Remove from the oven and let cool for about 10 minutes. Then, working in batches, rub them between the palms of your hands until the skins loosen and fall away. (This will take some time and not every bit of skin will rub off.)

In a large mixing bowl stir together the hazelnuts, flour, sugar, baking powder, baking soda, salt, almonds, and butter. In a separate bowl combine the whole eggs, egg yolk, vanilla, and orange zest and lightly beat with a fork until blended.

Add the egg mixture to the flour mixture and beat with a hand-held mixer set at medium speed until a granular dough forms. (This dough may overtax the motor of some hand-held mixers; if it does your mixer, beat the mixture only until it is a rough, shaggy mass, then knead it with flour-dusted hands in the bowl until all of the ingredients are well incorporated.)

Turn the dough out onto a lightly floured board and knead for 1 minute. Divide the dough into 4 equal portions. Using the palms of your hands, roll each portion into a log about 12 inches long and 1 inch in diameter.

Line a 12-inch-wide baking sheet that is at least 15 inches long with parchment paper or grease it with butter. Place the logs crosswise on the baking sheet, spacing them about 2 inches apart. Using the palm of one hand, lightly flatten the top of each log until it is about ½ inch thick.

Bake the logs in the preheated oven until golden brown, 15 to 20 minutes. Remove from the oven and let cool on the baking sheet until they can be handled, about 10 minutes. Leave the oven set at 350 degrees F.

Transfer the logs to a cutting board and cut them crosswise on the diagonal into pieces ½ inch wide. Line a second baking sheet with parchment paper or grease with butter. Arrange the pieces cut sides down on the 2 baking sheets. Return the cookies to the oven and bake until lightly toasted and the edges are golden brown, 10 minutes. Let cool completely on the baking sheets before serving. Store in a covered container at room temperature for up to 2 weeks.

½ cup whole raw hazelnuts

2 cups unbleached all-purpose flour

1 cup sugar

1 teaspoon baking powder

¼ teaspoon baking soda

⅛ teaspoon salt

½ cup whole raw almonds

3 tablespoons unsalted butter, at room temperature

2 whole eggs

1 egg yolk

1 teaspoon vanilla extract

2 teaspoons freshly grated orange zest

Additional flour for work surface

Additional unsalted butter for baking sheet (optional)

AMARETTI
Almond Macaroons

2¼ cups slivered blanched almonds, or 2½ cups blanched whole almonds

1 tablespoon cornstarch

1 cup powdered sugar

4 egg whites, at room temperature

⅛ teaspoon cream of tartar

¾ cup granulated sugar

½ tablespoon almond extract

Unsalted butter for baking sheets (optional)

Crystal sugar

The most famous amaretti come from Saronno, an industrial town north of Milan. They are packed in square tins, with each cookie individually wrapped in tissue-thin paper. Italians consume vast quantities of these light, crispy cookies for the festival of Santa Lucia, celebrated each December 14. On that day, children leave a basket filled with straw for Saint Lucy to feed her donkey. She gathers up the straw and then tucks a few amaretti and nougat candies (torrone) into the basket in a gesture of gratitude.

Preheat an oven to 300 degrees F.

Using a nut mill, blender, or a food processor fitted with the metal blade, grind the almonds to a fine powder. (If you are using a blender or processor, grind them with the cornstarch in small batches to keep them from releasing too much oil. If the almonds do become oily, pass them through a sieve to break up any lumps.) Place in a bowl. Add the cornstarch and powdered sugar, passing the sugar through a sieve to remove any lumps. Stir to mix and set aside.

Place the egg whites and cream of tartar in a large mixing bowl. Using a hand-held mixer set on low speed, beat the egg whites until they are frothy. Increase the speed to medium and continue to beat until soft peaks form, 3 to 4 minutes. Add about one fourth of the granulated sugar, increase the speed to high, and beat in until incorporated. Add the remaining sugar and continue beating until shiny, stiff peaks form. The process of beating the egg whites should take 4 to 5 minutes. Using a rubber spatula, gently fold in the almond extract and the almond mixture just until evenly distributed.

Line 2 baking sheets with parchment paper or grease them with butter. Spoon the egg white mixture into a pastry bag fitted with a No. 7 plain tip. Pipe out mounds 1 inch in diameter onto the prepared baking sheets, spacing the mounds about 1 inch apart. If necessary, flatten any peaks with a dampened pastry brush or index finger. Sprinkle the tops with crystal sugar.

Bake the cookies in the preheated oven until lightly and evenly browned, 35 to 40 minutes. Turn the oven off and leave the cookies in the oven to dry out for an additional 20 minutes. Using a metal spatula, gently remove to wire racks to cool completely. Store in a covered container at room temperature for up to 2 weeks. If humidity causes the cookies to become sticky, recrisp them in a preheated 250 degree F oven for 5 to 10 minutes.

ANICINI
Anise Cookies

These deep blond, aniseed-laced bars are found in pastry shops throughout Tuscany. Like cantucci, they are meant to be dipped, preferably into the region's renowned Vin Santo. But they are also delicious dunked in a glass of sweet Marsala or even a hearty red wine or port.

2⅓ cups unbleached all-purpose flour

1 teaspoon baking powder

¼ teaspoon salt

1 tablespoon aniseeds

1½ cups sliced raw almonds

¼ pound (1 stick) unsalted butter, at room temperature

1¼ cups sugar

3 eggs

½ teaspoon vanilla extract

¼ teaspoon anise extract

Additional flour for work surface

Additional unsalted butter for baking sheet (optional)

Preheat an oven to 375 degrees F.

In a bowl stir together the flour, baking powder, salt, aniseeds, and almonds. Set aside.

In a large mixing bowl, combine the butter and sugar. Using a hand-held mixer set on medium speed, beat the ingredients until the mixture is fluffy, light, and pale in color, about 5 minutes. Continuing to beat on medium speed, add the eggs, one at a time, beating well after each addition and scraping down the sides of the bowl with a rubber spatula. Beat in the vanilla and anise extracts. Reduce the speed to low and add the flour mixture, one third at a time, beating well after each addition until thoroughly incorporated. Beat until a smooth dough forms.

Turn the dough out onto a lightly floured work surface. Divide the dough into 4 equal portions. Using the palms of your hands, roll each portion into a log about 12 inches long and 1½ inches in diameter.

Line a 12-inch-wide baking sheet that is at least 18 inches long with parchment paper or grease it with butter. (Or use 2 baking sheets if you do not have one long enough; this dough spreads as it bakes.) Place the logs crosswise on the baking sheet, spacing them 3 inches apart. Using the palm of your hand, lightly flatten the top of each log until it is about ½ inch thick.

Bake the logs in the preheated oven until a light golden brown, about 18 minutes. Remove from the oven and let cool on the baking sheet(s) until they can be handled, about 10 minutes. Leave the oven set at 375 degrees F.

Transfer the logs to a cutting surface and, with a sharp knife, cut them crosswise on the diagonal into slices ½ inch wide. If a single sheet has been used to bake the logs, line a second baking sheet with parchment paper or grease it with butter. Arrange the pieces cut sides down on the baking sheet and return the cookies to the oven. Bake until nicely toasted and the edges are golden brown, 8 to 10 minutes. Let cool completely on the baking sheets before serving. Store in a covered container at room temperature for up to 2 weeks.

BISCOTTI DI ZUCCA
Pumpkin Cookies with Walnuts and Raisins

◆

MAKES ABOUT 4 DOZEN LARGE COOKIES

2¾ cups unbleached all-purpose flour

2 teaspoons baking powder

1 teaspoon baking soda

2 teaspoons ground cinnamon

1 teaspoon freshly grated nutmeg

1 teaspoon ground ginger

½ teaspoon ground cloves

¼ teaspoon salt

1¼ cups raisins

2 cups walnut pieces

½ pound (2 sticks) less 2 tablespoons unsalted butter, at room temperature

1 cup firmly packed brown sugar

2 eggs

1½ cups unseasoned canned pumpkin

Additional unsalted butter for baking sheets (optional)

For the glaze:

6 tablespoons (¾ stick) unsalted butter, melted and kept hot

1½ cups powdered sugar

This is actually an American cookie. In Italy pumpkin is used almost exclusively for making savories. My own nonna cooked wonderful tortelloni stuffed with pumpkin, a specialty of Mantua traditionally eaten on Christmas Eve with marinated eel.

These cookies burn easily on the bottom, so it is best to bake them one sheet at a time on the top rack in the oven. Be sure to purchase plain canned pumpkin and not preseasoned pie filling.

Preheat an oven to 375 degrees F.

Sift together the flour, baking powder and soda, cinnamon, nutmeg, ginger, cloves, and salt into a mixing bowl. Set aside. Combine the raisins and walnuts and set aside.

In a large mixing bowl, combine the butter and sugar. Using a hand-held mixer set on medium speed, beat the ingredients until the mixture is fluffy and light, about 5 minutes. Continuing to beat on medium speed, add the eggs, one at a time, beating well after each addition and scraping down the sides of the bowl with a rubber spatula. The mixture may look curdled, but do not worry. Beat in the pumpkin and mix just until combined. Reduce the speed to low and add the flour mixture, one third at a time, alternating with the raisin-walnut mixture, which should be added one half at a time. Beat well after each addition until thoroughly incorporated. The batter should be quite thick.

Line 2 baking sheets with parchment paper or grease them with butter. Drop the batter onto one of the prepared sheets by heaping tablespoonfuls, spacing the mounds about 1½ inches apart.

Bake the cookies in the top third of the preheated oven until browned on the bottom and the tops spring back when touched, 15 to 18 minutes. While the first batch is baking, load the second baking sheet. Remove the baked cookies to wire racks to cool completely.

To make the glaze, place the hot melted butter in a bowl and gradually whisk in the sugar with a wire whisk to form a smooth, flowing glaze that is not too thin. It should have the consistency of chocolate syrup. (If the glaze is too thick, whisk in a little milk or water.) Using a spoon drizzle the glaze over the tops of the cookies. (There may be a little glaze left over.) It will harden as it cools. Store in a covered container at room temperature for up to 1 week.

FAGOTTINI D'ALBICOCCA

Apricot Jam-Filled Pockets

❖

1 recipe Pasta Frolla
  dough (page 151)

Unsalted butter for bak-
  ing sheets (optional)

Unbleached all-purpose
  flour for work
  surface

2 eggs, lightly beaten

1 cup apricot jam

Plump, golden apricots — "eggs of the sun" as the Persians called them — appear in Italian mar-kets briefly during the warm days of summer. They are snatched up quickly and eaten while still blushing with color, or cooked into a jam for filling these crumbly "bundles."

Prepare the pastry dough, divide it in half, and chill both portions for at least 1 hour. Preheat an oven to 375 degrees F. Line 2 baking sheets with parchment paper or grease them with butter.

On a lightly floured work surface, roll out half of the chilled dough ¼ inch thick. Using a round plain cookie cutter 2½ inches in diameter, cut out as many rounds as possible. Lay the dough cutouts on a flat work surface. Gather up the scraps, reroll them, and again cut out as many 2½-inch rounds as possible. Do not reroll the dough again, as these scraps will produce cookies that are tough. Repeat with the remaining dough portion. You should have about 36 rounds in all.

Lightly brush each round with the beaten egg, then place a rounded teaspoon of apricot jam in the center of the round. Fold in half to form a half-moon and pinch the edges together to seal securely. Brush the top of each half-moon lightly with beaten egg.

Arrange the cookies 1 inch apart on the pre-pared sheets. Bake the cookies in the preheated oven until golden brown, 12 to 15 minutes. Remove to wire racks to cool completely before serving. Store in a covered container at room temperature for up to 1 week.

FAGOTTINI DI LAMPONE *Raspberry Jam-Filled Butter Cookies.* Substitute 1 cup raspberry jam for the apricot jam in *fagottini d'albicocca* and proceed as directed.

❖ ❖ ❖

BISCOTTI DI CRUSCA
Bran Cookies

◆

MAKES ABOUT 4 DOZEN COOKIES

Most Italians would question the very idea of a bran cookie. Indeed, my memories of crusca back home have nothing at all to do with the kitchen and everything to do with the farmyard. Putting it as delicately as possible, bran is what we fed to the animals. But now, under the influence of American taste and American bakers, I have come to appreciate this healthful biscotto, which is a favorite of many Il Fornaio regulars.

1 cup unbleached all-purpose flour

1 teaspoon baking soda

1 cup unprocessed wheat bran

¼ pound (1 stick) unsalted butter, at room temperature

1 cup sugar

1 egg

1 tablespoon dark rum

½ teaspoon vanilla extract

Additional unsalted butter for baking sheets (optional)

Additional flour for work surface

Preheat an oven to 350 degrees F. Sift together the flour and baking soda into a mixing bowl. Stir in the bran and set aside.

In a large mixing bowl, combine the butter and sugar. Using a hand-held mixer set on medium speed, beat the ingredients until the mixture is fluffy, light, and pale in color, about 5 minutes. Continuing to beat on medium speed, add the egg and beat thoroughly, scraping down the sides of the bowl with a rubber spatula. Beat in the rum and vanilla. Reduce the speed to low and add the flour mixture, one third at a time, beating well after each addition until thoroughly incorporated. The dough should be smooth except for the bran flecks.

Line 2 baking sheets with parchment paper or grease them with butter. Turn the dough out onto a lightly floured work surface. Divide the dough in half. Roll out half of the dough ¼ inch thick. Using a round plain or fluted cookie cutter 2½ inches in diameter, cut out as many rounds as possible. Arrange the cookies 1 inch apart on the prepared baking sheets. Gather up the scraps, reroll them, and again cut out as many 2½-inch rounds as possible. Do not reroll the dough again, as these scraps will produce cookies that are tough. Repeat with the remaining dough portion. Using the tines of a fork, prick each cookie several times.

Bake the cookies in the preheated oven until they are golden, firm, and give only slightly when touched in the center, 8 to 10 minutes. Remove to wire racks to cool completely. Store in a covered container at room temperature for up to 1 week.

BACI D'ALASSIO
Chocolate-Hazelnut Kisses

◆

Named for a Ligurian seaside town, baci d'Alassio are irresistible to anyone who has fallen under the spell of the rich chocolate confections for which northern Italy is famous. Baci means "kisses" and these hazelnut-laced cookies look like two Hershey chocolate baci caught in a passionate moment. The fanciful appellation these delectable mouthfuls go by comes as no surprise to Italians, for in Italy it is common to encounter chocolate treasures with names that link them with love.

You must plan ahead for these romantic cookies: The batter is piped onto sheets the day before the cookies go into the oven, to give the rosettes time to dry before baking. The recipe can be doubled, but piping the batter requires considerable strength and, if you tire before you have finished, it does not store well. Do not be tempted to use a larger pastry-bag tip, or the delicate edges of the cookies will be lost.

Preheat an oven to 350 degrees F.

Spread the hazelnuts in a single layer in a shallow pan and place them in the preheated oven, turning every now and again, until lightly toasted and the skins begin to blister, 15 to 18 minutes. Remove from the oven and let cool for 10 minutes. Then, working in batches, rub them between the palms of your hands until the skins loosen and fall away. (This will take some time and not every bit of skin will rub off.) Chop the hazelnuts coarsely.

Using a nut mill, blender, or a food processor fitted with the metal blade, grind the hazelnuts to a fine powder. (If the nuts do become oily, pass them through a sieve to break up any lumps.) Place in a large mixing bowl and stir in the sugar.

Add the butter, cocoa, honey, and vanilla and mix thoroughly with a wooden spoon. Add the egg whites, a little at a time, mixing well after each addition. Add only enough of the whites for the dough to take on the consistency of a loose paste or spritz cookie dough. Do not worry if all of the egg whites are not used.

Line 2 baking sheets with parchment paper or grease them with butter. Spoon the hazelnut mixture into a pastry bag fitted with a No. 6 star tip. Pipe out rosettes 1 inch in diameter onto the prepared sheets, spacing the rosettes about 1½ inches apart. You should have about 60 rosettes in all. Let the rosettes sit, uncovered, at room temperature overnight.

Preheat an oven to 375 degrees F. Bake the cookies in the preheated oven until firm to the touch but still moist inside, 8 to 10 minutes. When they are done they will not be brown and may even look undercooked, so you must test by touch. Remove to wire racks to cool completely.

Meanwhile, melt the chocolate in the top pan of a double boiler placed over simmering water. Remove from the heat and let cool to room temperature, stirring occasionally. Gently turn half of the cookies top sides down on a flat surface and spread about ½ teaspoon chocolate on each of the upturned bottoms. As each cookie is coated, press a plain cookie onto the chocolate, bottom side down, to form a "sandwich." Lay the cookies on their sides on a tray or flat plate and refrigerate for 15 minutes to set the chocolate. Store in a covered container at room temperature for up to 1 week.

3 cups whole raw hazelnuts

2 cups sugar

2 tablespoons unsalted butter, melted

½ cup Dutch-process unsweetened cocoa powder, sieved

1 tablespoon honey

2 teaspoons vanilla extract

4 or 5 egg whites, at room temperature

Additional unsalted butter for baking sheets (optional)

3 ounces semisweet chocolate

BISCOTTI ALLE MANDORLE
Almond Cookies

◆

1 recipe Pasta Frolla
dough (page 151)

3 eggs

10 ounces natural
almond paste

Unsalted butter for bak-
ing sheets (optional)

Unbleached all-purpose
flour for work
surface

About 80 blanched
almond halves (about
1¼ cups)

Italian bakers use smooth, rich almond paste in scores of sweets. Although purists may insist upon mixing ground almonds, corn syrup, and sugar together to make their own pasta di mandorle, I suggest buying a good-quality commercial product. Look for almond paste in specialty-food shops and better supermarkets. Here, the sweet nut paste is concealed between layers of butter-rich dough to form a simple cookie customarily baked during the Easter season.

Prepare the dough, divide it in half, and chill both portions for at least 1 hour. Preheat an oven to 350 degrees F.

In a mixing bowl lightly beat 2 of the eggs. Add the almond paste and, using a sturdy wooden spoon, break it up into small pieces. Then, using a hand-held mixer set on medium speed, beat together only until the eggs are incorporated. Avoid beating too much air into the mixture or the cookies will rise too much during baking. Alternatively, stir the eggs and almond paste together using a wooden spoon.

Line 2 baking sheets with parchment paper or grease them with butter. On a lightly floured work surface, roll out half of the chilled dough ¼ inch thick. Using a round plain cookie cutter 3 inches in diameter, cut out as many rounds as possible on half of the pastry sheet. Using a round fluted cookie cutter 3 inches in diameter, cut out an equal number of rounds on the remaining half of the sheet. Place a heaping spoonful of the almond mixture in the center of each plain round, then flatten the mixture slightly. Top each filled plain round with a fluted round and gently pinch the edges together. Arrange the cookies on a prepared sheet, spacing the rounds about 1½ inches apart. Gather up the scraps, reroll them, again cut out an equal number of plain and fluted rounds, and fill them. Do not reroll the dough again, as these scraps will produce cookies that are tough. Repeat with the remaining dough portion.

In a small bowl beat the remaining egg. Brush the tops of the cookies with the beaten egg and arrange 4 almond halves in a star pattern on top of each.

Bake the cookies in the preheated oven until golden brown, 10 to 12 minutes. Remove to wire racks to cool completely. Store in a covered container at room temperature for up to 1 week.

BISCOTTI DA TÈ

Butter Cookies

MAKES ABOUT TWO DOZEN COOKIES

Biscotti da tè — *literally, "tea cookies" — are buttery confections that are baked either plain or topped with a fruit jam. One of my sisters married a man from Rome, where no one would think of serving a butter cookie without a crown of jam. In Lazio, the countryside surrounding the Eternal City, people pick wild berries just for this purpose. I have included variations using raspberry and apricot jams, but almost any favorite fruit preserve will do.*

Sift the flour into a bowl and set aside.

In a large mixing bowl, combine the butter and sugar. Using a hand-held mixer set on medium speed, beat the ingredients until the mixture is fluffy, light, and pale in color, about 5 minutes. Continuing to beat on medium speed, add the whole egg and beat thoroughly, scraping down the sides of the bowl with a rubber spatula. Add the egg yolk, vanilla, lemon zest or extract, and salt and beat until combined. Reduce the speed to low and add the flour, one third at a time, beating well after each addition until thoroughly incorporated. The dough will be smooth but somewhat dry.

Turn the dough out onto a lightly floured work surface and knead 2 or 3 times. Flatten slightly into a disk, wrap tightly, and refrigerate for about 1 hour. Meanwhile, preheat an oven to 350 degrees F.

Line 2 baking sheets with parchment paper or grease them with butter. On a lightly floured work surface, roll out the dough ½ inch thick. Using a round fluted cookie cutter 2½ inches in diameter, cut out as many rounds as possible. Arrange the cookies on the prepared sheets, spacing the rounds about 1 inch apart (these cookies spread as they bake, more so on the bottom than on the top). Gather up the scraps, reroll them, and again cut out as many 2½-inch rounds as possible. Do not reroll the dough again, as these scraps will produce cookies that are tough.

Bake the cookies in the preheated oven until pale blond and firm to the touch, 12 to 15 minutes. Remove to wire racks to cool completely. Store in a covered container at room temperature for up to 1 week.

FROLLETTE DI LAMPONE O D'ALBICOCCA
Butter Cookies Filled with Raspberry or Apricot Jam.
Prepare the *biscotti da tè* through the point at which they are arranged on baking sheets. Make a shallow indentation in the center of each cookie and spoon ½ teaspoon raspberry or apricot jam into each hollow. You will need a generous ¼ cup jam in all. Bake and store as directed.

3 cups unbleached all purpose flour

½ pound (2 sticks) plus 2 tablespoons unsalted butter, at room temperature

1 cup sugar

1 whole egg

1 egg yolk

½ teaspoon vanilla extract

Grated zest of 1 lemon, or ½ teaspoon lemon extract

Pinch of salt

Additional flour for work surface

Additional unsalted butter for baking sheets (optional)

MEINI
Sweet Cornmeal Buns

◆

MAKES 12 BUNS

Bakers near Lake Como specialize in these sugar-topped pale gold buns. Sweets made with cornmeal are often prepared in the fall, especially around the *Festi di Santi Morti* at the beginning of November, because fewer fresh ingredients are available in the cool months. The term un meino is used to describe something round; in Lombardy the word is slang for money — a round, golden coin.

Preheat an oven to 375 degrees F.

Sift together the flour, baking powder, and cornmeal into a mixing bowl. Set aside.

In a large mixing bowl, combine the butter, sugar, and honey. Using a hand-held mixer set on medium speed, beat the ingredients together until the mixture is fluffy, light, and pale in color, about 5 minutes. Continuing to beat on medium speed, add the egg yolks, one at a time, beating well after each addition and scraping down the sides of the bowl with a rubber spatula.

Reduce the speed to low, add half of the flour mixture, and beat until the dry ingredients are thoroughly incorporated. Beat in the cream, milk, lemon zest, and vanilla. Continuing to mix on low speed, add the remaining flour mixture and beat until a soft dough forms, about 2 minutes.

Turn the dough out onto a lightly floured work surface. The dough will be sticky, but try not to incorporate too much flour as you shape the buns. Divide the dough into 12 equal portions.

Dust your hands lightly with flour and shape each portion into a golfball-sized sphere. With the palm of one hand, flatten each ball slightly on the floured surface into a disk about ¾ inch thick.

Line a baking sheet with parchment paper or grease it with butter. To decorate the tops of the buns, put the granulated sugar into a small, shallow bowl. Brush the top of each disk lightly with water and then dip the dampened top into the granulated sugar. Place the disks, sugared sides up, on the prepared baking sheet, spacing them about 2 inches apart. When all of the disks have been dipped, sieve the powdered sugar over the tops.

Bake the buns in the preheated oven until the tops begin to crack and the rim of each bun is a light golden brown, 15 to 18 minutes. Remove from the oven and let cool completely on the baking sheet. Store in a covered container at room temperature for up to 5 days.

1⅓ cups unbleached all-purpose flour

2 teaspoons baking powder

1 cup fine-grind yellow cornmeal

¼ pound plus 4 table-spoons (1½ sticks) unsalted butter, at room temperature

½ cup sugar

2 tablespoons honey

2 egg yolks

¼ cup whipping cream

¼ cup milk

1½ teaspoons freshly grated lemon zest

½ teaspoon vanilla extract

Additional flour for work surface

Additional unsalted butter for baking sheet (optional)

For the tops:

½ cup granulated sugar

½ cup powdered sugar

PINOLATE

Pine Nut Cookies

———————◆———————

MAKES ABOUT 3 DOZEN COOKIES

I*n Italy, pine nuts are harvested from cones of the Italian stone pine. Separating the rich, ivory "seeds" from the cones' crevices is slow work, which accounts for the high cost of* pinoli. *These pale golden cookies with their spiky nut coats recall chewy macaroons.*

1½ cups slivered blanched almonds, or 1¾ cups blanched whole almonds

1½ cups sugar

3 egg whites, at room temperature

⅛ teaspoon cream of tartar

¼ teaspoon almond extract

Unsalted butter for baking sheets (optional)

3 to 4 cups pine nuts

Preheat an oven to 375 degrees F.

Using a nut mill, blender, or a food processor fitted with a metal blade, grind the almonds to a fine powder. (If you are using a blender or food processor, grind them with 6 tablespoons of the sugar in small batches to keep them from releasing too much oil. If the almonds do become oily, pass them through a sieve to break up any lumps.) Set aside.

Place the egg whites and cream of tartar in a medium-sized mixing bowl. Using a hand-held mixer set on low speed, beat the egg whites until they are frothy. Increase the speed to medium and continue to beat until soft peaks form, 3 to 4 minutes. Add about one fourth of the sugar, increase the speed to high, and beat in. Add the remaining sugar and continue beating until shiny, stiff peaks form. The process of beating the egg whites should take 4 to 5 minutes in all. Using a rubber spatula, gently fold in the almond extract and the ground almonds just until evenly distributed. The mixture will have the consistency of very dense, stiffly beaten egg whites.

Line 2 large baking sheets with parchment paper or grease them with butter. Spread the pine nuts in a large shallow baking dish (the layer should be several nuts deep). Dip a tablespoon in cold water, scoop up a spoonful of the batter, and drop it onto the nuts. Repeat, dipping the spoon in water each time and dropping several spoonfuls of batter onto the dish in the same manner, making sure that they do not touch. Then, using your fingers roll the mounds of batter around in the nuts, coating them evenly and pressing the nuts on firmly. Arrange the mounds on a prepared baking sheet, spacing them about 2 inches apart. Repeat until you have filled one of the baking sheets completely.

Bake the cookies in the top third of the preheated oven. They are done when the nuts are golden, the cookies are light brown and firm to the touch, and the insides are still chewy, 15 to 18 minutes. While the first batch is baking, load the second baking sheet. Remove the baked cookies to wire racks to cool completely. Store in a covered container at room temperature for up to 2 weeks.

PASTA FROLLA
Short Pastry Dough

◆

This butter-rich pastry, which crumbles deliciously in the mouth, is the base for a myriad of Italian sweets, from the raisin-laden Garibaldi cookie to a variety of fruit-filled tarts. The recipe yields enough dough to make two ten-inch tarts. When you roll it out, note the thickness specified in the recipe. It is important that a tart shell not be too thick, so you may find yourself rolling a larger round than is necessary to line the pan. The pastry scraps can be used for making a few small sugar-dusted cookies. Do not reroll the scraps more than once, however, because the dough will toughen. This dough also can be frozen, well wrapped, for up to two weeks. Thaw overnight in the refrigerator before using.

2 cups unbleached all-purpose flour

½ cup sugar

¼ teaspoon salt

¼ pound plus 6 tablespoons (1¾ sticks) unsalted butter, at room temperature

1 whole egg

1 egg yolk

¾ teaspoon vanilla extract

½ teaspoon lemon extract

Additional flour for work surface and hands

In a large mixing bowl, combine the flour, sugar, salt, and butter. Using a hand-held mixer set on low speed, beat until the mixture is crumbly and forms pea-sized balls.

In a separate bowl combine the whole egg, egg yolk, and vanilla and lemon extracts and lightly beat together with a fork. Add the egg mixture to the flour mixture and beat on low speed until a rough, shaggy mass forms.

Turn the dough out onto a lightly floured work surface. Dust your hands with flour and knead the dough until it is smooth and all the ingredients are thoroughly incorporated, about 1 minute. Wrap and chill for at least 1 hour before using, or store for up to 4 days.

If chilled for longer than 1 hour, the dough will be quite hard. Let it warm *slightly* before beginning to work with it. You can press on it a few times with a rolling pin to make it more malleable. Do not handle it too much or it will bake up tough.

GARIBALDI
Raisin-Filled Butter Cookies

MAKES 42 COOKIES

Throughout Italy there are countless statues and piazzas named after Giuseppe Garibaldi, the nineteenth-century revolutionary who led an army of irregulars on what proved to be his crowning military enterprise — the 1860 liberation of the Two Sicilies. These typically Milanese cookies of buttery dough layers encasing sweet golden raisins were named for the great Italian patriot by Il Fornaio. The reasoning was simple: A raisin-packed Garibaldi gives you the energy to charge forward, the same energy that pushed Garibaldi to overthrow the Bourbons.

◆ ◆ ◆

Prepare the pastry dough, divide it in half, and chill both portions for at least 1 hour.

Caramelize the sugar by placing it in a small, heavy saucepan over high heat. Watch the pan closely to avoid burning the sugar. The sugar will begin to melt and then gradually turn from a clear liquid to a dark brown. At this point add the water, standing away from the pan in case the cold liquid causes the hot sugar to bubble and splatter. Lower the heat to medium and continue cooking until the mixture is syrupy, about 1 minute. Remove from the heat and set aside to cool.

Select a 9-by-13-inch baking sheet with ⅝-inch sides. Line it with parchment paper cut to fit the bottom of the pan precisely or grease it with butter. Set aside.

On a lightly floured work surface, roll out half of the chilled dough into a rectangle that is the exact dimensions of the baking sheet bottom. Place the rolling pin across one end of the pastry rectangle and loosely roll the pastry around the pin. Unroll the pastry onto the prepared baking sheet and press it gently onto the bottom.

Brush the surface of the dough lightly with some of the egg. Sprinkle the raisins over the entire surface of dough and then, using the rolling pin, lightly press them into the dough. Brush the tops of the raisins thoroughly with all but ¼ cup of the remaining beaten egg.

Roll out the remaining dough to the same dimensions as the first half and transfer it in the same manner to the baking sheet. Roll the rolling pin lightly over the dough to press it lightly against the raisins. Stir the remaining ¼ cup beaten egg into the caramelized sugar and brush the egg mixture over the entire surface of the dough. Run the tines of a large fork or a cake-decorating comb crosswise atop the pastry in a wavy pattern that covers the entire surface. Let this coating dry at room temperature until barely tacky, about 30 minutes, depending upon the humidity in the room. Then cover the baking sheet and slip the dough in the freezer until it feels quite hard to the touch, about 2 hours.

Preheat an oven to 375 degrees F. Gently pry the dough away from the pan and place it on a lightly floured work surface. (Freezing the dough makes this step easy.) With a sharp knife trim off as little dough as possible from each side to form even edges. Cut the dough lengthwise into 6 strips, each about 1½ inches wide. Then cut each strip crosswise into 7 equal bars.

Line 1 large baking sheet or 2 smaller ones with parchment paper or grease with butter. Arrange the bars on the sheet, spacing them 1 inch apart. Bake the bars in the preheated oven until the tops are deep brown and the bottoms are light brown, 12 to 15 minutes. Let cool completely on the baking sheet(s) before serving. Store in a covered container at room temperature for up to 1 week.

1 recipe Pasta Frolla dough (page 151)

2 tablespoons sugar

1½ tablespoons water

Unsalted butter for baking sheet (optional)

Unbleached all-purpose flour for work surface

2 eggs, lightly beaten

2¼ cups golden raisins

DOLCI

Sweets

*A*lmost every Italian town, no matter how small, has at least one — and usually more — *pasticcerie* selling *crostate, torte,* and other delectable sweets. The Italian passion for *dolci* is so intense that no holiday passes without the prescribed sweet being served, whether it is *cucciddati,* the date-stuffed pastry prepared for the Sicilian feast of San Giuseppe, or *torta primavera,* the dense yellow cake that accompanies a Lombardian Easter.

At the Panificio d'Alba we stoked the furnace before dawn and baked the breads in the morning when the oven heat was fiercest. In the afternoon the temperature cooled to the point where it was perfect for the cakes and tarts. I learned to make fresh fruit *crostate* and a butter-rich *pan d'angeli,* and we baked a resolutely old-fashioned *torta secca* of flour, cornmeal, lard, sugar, lemon, and vanilla that I still crave today.

The *panificio* was particularly well-known for its cakes. We had the reputation for making the finest wedding *torte* for miles around, and people loved our sponge cake, which I iced with a luscious sweet fondant sugar. Because home ovens were a novelty in those days, local women would bring their own unbaked cakes into the bakery, and I would slip them in alongside whatever we were baking and receive a few *lire* for my trouble.

The *dolci* you find here are confirmation that Italian bakers appreciate both the simple and the elaborate. There is the unpretentious cornmeal cake called *amor di polenta* and the rosette-crowned *gianduia,* a Turinese construction rich with chocolate and hazelnuts. Although some of the most famous Italian sweets originated in Sicily, most of the *dolci* from the Il Fornaio ovens — and in this chapter — come from the north of Italy.

AMOR DI POLENTA
Cornmeal Cake

In Lombardy's Bergamo Province, this cake is commonly baked in a dome shape that recalls the traditional serving form of its savory cousin, polenta. *The winsome name is the result of an old Italian custom: when something is thought of as wonderful or sweet or a beauty, it is called* un amore, *"a love." At Il Fornaio we honor the name by baking the light, crumbly cake in a heart-shaped pan. It is lovely served without any adornment.*

½ cup cake flour

½ cup fine-grind yellow cornmeal

1 teaspoon baking powder

¼ pound (1 stick) plus 3 tablespoons unsalted butter, at room temperature

1¼ cups powdered sugar

¼ cup natural almond paste

4 egg yolks

2 whole eggs

½ teaspoon almond extract

⅛ teaspoon vanilla extract

Additional unsalted butter and cornmeal for loaf pan

Additional powdered sugar for cake top

Preheat an oven to 350 degrees F.

Sift together the flour, cornmeal, and baking powder into a large mixing bowl. Set aside.

In another large mixing bowl, combine the butter, sugar, and almond paste. Using a hand-held mixer set on medium speed, beat the ingredients until the mixture is very fluffy, light, and pale in color, 6 to 8 minutes. Continuing to beat on medium speed, add the egg yolks, one at a time, and then the whole eggs, one at a time, mixing well after each addition and scraping down the sides of the bowl with a rubber spatula. Beat in the almond and vanilla extracts. Reduce the speed to low and add the flour mixture, one third at a time, beating well after each addition until thoroughly incorporated.

Grease an 8½-by-4½-by-2½-inch loaf pan with butter and then sprinkle with cornmeal. Pour the batter into the pan. It is not necessary to level the surface.

Bake the cake in the preheated oven until golden brown and a wooden toothpick inserted in the center comes out dry, about 45 minutes. Remove from the oven and let the cake cool in the pan for 15 minutes, then, while it is still warm, turn it out onto a wire rack and let cool completely. Sieve a light dusting of powdered sugar over the top before serving. Store tightly wrapped at room temperature for up to 3 days.

TORTA MADDALENA
Sponge Cake

◆

MAKES ONE 8 1/2-INCH CAKE; SERVES 8

This light cake, which is similar to a French génoise, is the base for a number of desserts, including tiramisù *(page 160) and* torta d'Amaretto *(page 166). How it came by its name I am not sure. But Italians often name dishes after saints, so perhaps it honors Santa Maria Maddalena.*

Preheat an oven to 350 degrees F.

Grease an 8½-inch springform pan with 2-inch sides with butter. Cut out a round of parchment paper to fit the bottom precisely. Slip the paper into the pan. Sift together the cake flour and baking powder into a mixing bowl and set it aside as well.

In the top pan of a double boiler placed over simmering water, whisk the whole eggs, egg yolks, sugar, honey and lemon zest continuously until the mixture is hot to the touch, about 120 degrees F. Pour the hot egg mixture into a large mixing bowl and beat with a hand-held mixer set on high speed until the mixture triples in volume and is mousselike in texture, about 10 minutes.

Pour the flour mixture back into the sifter and sift it over the top of the egg mixture. Using a wire whisk combine the dry ingredients and the wet ingredients with a folding motion: gently move from the top to the bottom of the batter in a continuous action until no lumps remain.

Pour the batter into the prepared pan and bake in the preheated oven until a wooden toothpick inserted in the center comes out dry, 30 to 40 minutes. Remove from the oven and let the cake cool in the pan for 5 minutes.

Run a thin-bladed knife between the pan sides and cake and then unclasp and lift off the pan sides. Let the cake cool for 10 more minutes, then remove the pan bottom and peel off the paper. Set on a wire rack to cool completely.

This cake can be well wrapped and stored in the refrigerator for up to 4 days.

TORTA MADDALENA AL CIOCCOLATO
Chocolate Sponge Cake. Substitute ¼ cup Dutch-process unsweetened cocoa powder for ¼ cup of the cake flour in the *torta Maddalena.*

Unsalted butter for cake pan

1 cup cake flour

¼ teaspoon baking powder

3 whole eggs

3 egg yolks

⅔ cup sugar

1½ tablespoons honey

1 teaspoon freshly grated lemon zest

HOW OLD IS
TIRAMISU?

◆

A second tale of
tiramisù's origin
expands its history far
beyond a decade and a
half and puts its creation
in a different region.
According to this
account, the dessert was
concocted to celebrate the
arrival of Grand Duke
Cosimo de' Medici III
in the lovely Tuscan
town of Siena at the
beginning of the
eighteenth century. It
was named zuppa del
duca, the "duke's soup,"
and Cosimo III liked it
so much that he carried
the recipe home to
Florence. Later it became
all the fashion in the
British expatriate
community. And, so the
story goes, the British
carried the recipe back to
England, where it was
transformed into the
trifle. It is a wonderful
tale, in part because it
comes to us from none
other than Lorenza de'
Medici, a descendant of
the grand duke and
today one of Italy's best-
known food writers.

TIRAMISÙ
"Pick Me Up"

◆

MAKES ONE 9-INCH CAKE; SERVES 12 TO 14

In the 1980s tiramisù *became* di rigore *on Italian restaurant menus throughout the world — a rapid rise to fame considering the dessert's relatively short fifteen-year history. Similar to an English trifle or the Sicilian* zuppa inglese, *tiramisù originated in the region of Friuli-Venezia Giulia and its components vary slightly from kitchen to kitchen. In this version rich sponge-cake layers are sprinkled with espresso and rum, stacked with* mascarpone *cream and* zabaglione, *and then dusted with cocoa powder. (Mascarpone, a rich fresh cheese from Lombardy that is sometimes eaten alone for dessert with just a sprinkle of sugar or splash of liqueur, is available in Italian delicatessens and well-stocked supermarkets.)*

The dessert's unusual name derives from an Italian morning ritual of going into a caffè *and asking the barkeep for a tiramisù, something to "pick me up." A shot of rich, thick Vov is poured, which gives the drinker energy. Vov is made from eggs, sugar, and Marsala, the same ingredients that go into the zabaglione that enriches the best* tiramisù.

Prepare the *torta* and let cool to room temperature.

To make the *zabaglione*, in the top pan of a large double boiler off the heat, beat together the egg yolks and sugar with a hand-held mixer on high speed or a wire whisk until lemon colored and creamy, about 5 minutes. Set over barely simmering water. Add the Marsala and continue to beat until the mixture triples in volume and holds soft peaks, about 3 minutes.

Remove from the heat and continue mixing on high speed until the mixture has cooled slightly, about 5 minutes. You should have about 2 cups; set aside.

To make the *mascarpone* cream, place the cheese in a small bowl and, using a hand-held mixer set on medium speed, beat until smooth. With clean beaters, in a large bowl beat the cream with a hand-held mixer set on medium speed until it holds soft peaks. Add the whipped cheese, sugar, egg yolk, and vanilla extract to the cream and continue to beat on medium speed until the mixture holds stiff peaks. You should have about 3¼ cups; set aside.

To make the coffee mixture, combine the espresso, sugar, and rum in a small bowl and stir well to dissolve the coffee and sugar.

To assemble the *tiramisù*, using a sharp serrated knife, slice the *torta* horizontally into 3 equal layers. Place one of the cake layers in a shallow, flat-bottomed casserole or bowl, preferably of clear glass, 9 inches or a little larger in diameter. Brush one third of the coffee mixture evenly over the layer. Spread one third of the *mascarpone* cream on top and then spread one third of the *zabaglione* on top of the cream. Repeat with the remaining layers, coffee mixture, *mascarpone* cream, and *zabaglione* to make three layers, ending with *zabaglione*. Sieve cocoa powder evenly over the top.

Cover and refrigerate at least 4 hours to blend flavors. The cake may be stored, refrigerated, for up to 3 days. To serve, cut into wedges or spoon onto dessert plates.

NOTE   If you are unable to brew espresso, in its place use 1½ tablespoons instant coffee dissolved in ½ cup boiling water.

1 recipe Torta Maddalena *(page 159)*

For the *zabaglione:*

4 egg yolks

¼ cup sugar

¼ cup sweet Marsala

For the *mascarpone* cream:

1 cup (8 ounces) mascarpone *cheese*

1¼ cups whipping cream

6 tablespoons powdered sugar

1 egg yolk

½ teaspoon vanilla extract

For the coffee mixture:

½ cup freshly brewed espresso *(see Note)*

1 tablespoon sugar

½ cup dark rum

Dutch-process unsweetened cocoa powder for top

GIANDUIA
Chocolate Sponge Cake with Chocolate-Hazelnut Cream

The medieval Piedmontese town of Alba is famous for the pricy, pungent white truffles harvested each year from September through January in the nearby forest glades. It is also the headquarters of Ferrero, the world's best-known and largest purveyor of hazelnut cream, a soft, rich chocolate-and-nut spread that Italian schoolchildren slather on bread much the same way American youngsters eat peanut butter. The Ferrero label, Nutella, appears on jars in well-stocked supermarkets and food-specialty shops.

1 recipe Torta Maddalena al Cioccolato *omitting the lemon zest (page 159)*

¾ cup whole raw hazelnuts

2 tablespoons Frangelico liqueur (optional)

1 cup whipping cream, well chilled

½ cup Nutella hazelnut cream

Powdered sugar for top

Prepare the *torta* and let cool to room temperature. Preheat an oven to 350 degrees F. Chill a mixing bowl in the freezer for about 15 minutes.

Spread the hazelnuts in a single layer in a shallow pan and place them in the preheated oven, turning every now and again, until lightly toasted and the skins begin to blister, 15 to 18 minutes. Remove from the oven and let cool for about 10 minutes, then, working in 2 or 3 batches, rub them between the palms of your hands until the skins loosen and fall away. (This will take some time and not every bit of skin will rub off.) Reserve 8 to 10 perfectly peeled hazelnuts for decoration. Using a chef's knife, coarsely chop the remaining nuts.

Using a sharp serrated knife, cut the *torta* in half horizontally to form 2 layers. Place the bottom half on a cake platter and set the top half aside. If desired, brush the bottom with the liqueur.

Pour the cream into the chilled bowl. Using a wire whisk or a hand-held mixer set at medium speed, whip the cream until firm peaks just begin to form; do not overwhip. This should take 60 to 70 seconds with a whisk, or about 45 seconds with a mixer. Using a rubber spatula, gently fold in the Nutella, mixing until there are no streaks. Set aside half of the cream mixture. Fold the chopped hazelnuts into the remaining half and spread the mixture over the cake bottom, extending it to within ½ inch of the edge. Cover with the cake top and press gently to spread the cream even with the edge of the cake.

Sieve a thin layer of powdered sugar over the top of the cake. Spoon the remaining cream mixture into a pastry bag fitted with a No. 6 star tip and pipe 8 to 10 rosettes around the top edge of the cake. Place a whole hazelnut on each rosette. Chill before serving, but for no more than 3 hours.

TORTA D'ALASSIO
Chocolate Cake with Hazelnuts and Honey

MAKES ONE 8-INCH CAKE; SERVES 10

Alassio is a wonderful town on the Ligurian coast between Genoa and the French border, and in the summer its beaches are covered with Italian sunbathers. When I was a teenager, every July my friends and I would talk of going to the beach at Alassio to see the beautiful women.

This cake was dubbed torta d'Alassio *by Il Fornaio, and at the bakery we sometimes inscribe "Alassio" across the top. It is a rich chocolate sponge cake with an equally rich chocolate glaze — very beautiful, just like the bathers on the Alassio beaches.*

◆ ◆ ◆

The fertile Langhe hills near Alba, in the Piedmont, are covered with hazelnut groves. The nuts there are reputed particularly aromatic and are much sought after by those who make the classic dolci *of the region — from nut-rich* torte *to the crunchy nougat confection* torrone *— and beyond.*

Some authorities believe that the skins on the hazelnuts cultivated in the Alban hills slip off more easily than those of hazelnuts grown elsewhere. You may wish you had some Piedmontese nuts when you try to separate the kernels from their papery skins, for it can be a tedious task. Some cooks recommend wrapping the cooled toasted hazelnuts in a towel for the rubbing step to make the process easier.

Preheat an oven to 350 degrees F.

Grease an 8-inch-round cake pan with butter. Cut out a round of parchment paper to fit the pan bottom precisely and slip the paper into the pan. Set aside.

Spread the hazelnuts in a single layer in a shallow pan and place them in the preheated oven, turning every now and again, until they are lightly toasted and the skins begin to blister, 15 to 18 minutes. Remove from the oven and leave the oven set at 350 degrees F. Let the nuts cool for 10 minutes, then, working in batches, rub them between the palms of your hands until the skins loosen and fall away. (This will take some time and not every bit of skin will rub off.) Set ½ cup of the hazelnuts aside.

Using a nut mill, blender, or a food processor fitted with the metal blade, grind the remaining ¾ cup hazelnuts to a fine powder. (If you are using a blender or food processor, grind them in small batches to keep them from releasing too much oil. If the nuts do become oily, pass them through a sieve to break up any lumps.) Set aside.

In the top pan of a double boiler placed over gently simmering water, heat the chocolate until melted. Set aside to cool.

In a large mixing bowl, combine the butter and ½ cup of the sugar. Using a hand-held mixer set on medium speed, beat the ingredients until the mixture is very fluffy, light, and pale in color, 6 to 8 minutes. Continuing to beat on medium speed, add the egg yolks, one at a time, beating well after each addition. Reduce the speed to low and beat in the melted chocolate and ground hazelnuts. Throughout the mixing process, stop and scrape down the bowl sides several times with a rubber spatula to make sure the ingredients are well incorporated. Set aside.

In a separate mixing bowl, place the egg whites and, using clean beaters, beat them on high speed until they hold soft peaks. With the beaters engaged, gradually add the remaining ¼ cup sugar and continue to beat until the whites once again hold soft peaks.

Using a rubber spatula, fold half of the egg whites into the chocolate mixture. Then fold in the flour and finally the remaining egg whites.

Pour the batter into the prepared pan and bake in the preheated oven until the cake is firm to the touch, about 35 minutes. Remove from the oven and cool in the pan until barely warm, then invert onto a wire rack to cool completely.

To make the glaze, melt together the chocolate, butter, and honey in the top pan of a double boiler placed over simmering water. All the ingredients should be fully melted and blended together but not too hot; the glaze should feel warm to the touch. Do not heat it too much or it will be too thin. Pour the warm glaze over the top of the cooled cake; it should run down the sides.

Coarsely chop the reserved hazelnuts and, with your fingertips, press them onto the sides of the cake. Serve with whipped cream on the side, if desired.

Unsalted butter for cake pan

1¼ cups whole raw hazelnuts

8 ounces bittersweet chocolate, coarsely chopped

¼ pound (1 stick) unsalted butter, at room temperature

¾ cup sugar

3 eggs, separated

¼ cup unbleached all-purpose flour, sifted

For the chocolate glaze:

4 ounces bittersweet chocolate

¼ pound (1 stick) unsalted butter

1 tablespoon honey

Whipped cream for serving (optional)

TORTA D'AMARETTO
Sponge Cake with Chantilly Cream and Crushed Almond Cookies

◆

1 recipe Torta
Maddalena (page
159)

2 tablespoons Amaretto
liqueur (optional)

25 to 35 homemade
(page 138) or store-
bought amaretti
(4 or 5 ounces)

1 cup whipping cream,
well chilled

1 tablespoon powdered
sugar

Additional powdered
sugar for top

The stones of apricots give the almond-flavored Amaretto liqueur used in this classic Lombardian cake its pleasantly sharp bouquet. If you have no homemade amaretti on hand and lack the time to bake them, try a local pasticerria or buy a box of the legendary almond cookies imported from the amaretti capital, Saronno.

Prepare the *torta* and let cool to room temperature. Chill a mixing bowl in the freezer for about 15 minutes.

Using a sharp serrated knife, cut the *torta* in half horizontally to form 2 layers. Place four 3-inch-wide strips of waxed paper along the edges of the cake platter. Place the cake bottom on the platter; the waxed-paper strips should be half-covered by the cake. Set the top half aside. If desired, brush the bottom with the liqueur.

Place the *amaretti* in a plastic bag and, using a rolling pin, crush them to crumbs. The crumbs will be uneven; some may be quite fine, while others will be coarser. Crush any crumbs that are larger than ¼ inch. There should be about 1 cup crumbs.

Pour the cream into the chilled bowl and add the powdered sugar. Using a wire whisk or a hand-held mixer set at medium speed, whip the cream until firm peaks just begin to form; do not overwhip. This should take 60 to 70 seconds with a whisk, or about 45 seconds with a mixer. Using a rubber spatula, gently fold in two thirds of the crushed cookies, then set aside one third of the cream-cookie mixture. Spread the remaining mixture over the cake bottom, extending it to within ½ inch of the edge. Cover with the cake top and press gently to spread the cream even with the edge of the cake.

Using a rubber spatula or a metal icing spatula, spread the reserved cream mixture onto the sides of the cake. Then, using your fingertips, press the reserved crumbs onto the sides. (This amount of crumbs will coat the cake lightly. If you prefer a heavier coating, add more crumbs.) Sieve a thin layer of powdered sugar over the top. Remove the waxed-paper strips, taking with them any fallen cream and crumbs. Chill before serving, but for no more than 3 hours.

TORTA SAVOIA
Chocolate Marble Pound Cake

MAKES ONE 9-INCH CAKE; SERVES 10 TO 12

Since the sixteenth century, when cocoa beans were first carried from the New World to the Old, Turinese bakers have been producing cakes in all shapes, sizes, and degrees of chocolate intensity. This simple torta, made with marbleized white and chocolate batters, was one of their earliest creations and remains one of the easiest to make and most satisfying to eat.

Unsalted butter and unbleached all-purpose flour for tube pan

2 ounces bittersweet or semisweet chocolate

1¼ cups unbleached all-purpose flour

1 teaspoon baking powder

¼ pound (1 stick) plus 2 tablespoons unsalted butter, at room temperature

1¼ cups sugar

5 eggs

1 teaspoon vanilla extract

Grated zest of 1 lemon

Preheat an oven to 350 degrees F. Butter and flour a 9-inch tube pan with a 2-quart capacity.

In the top pan of a double boiler placed over simmering water, heat the chocolate until melted; keep warm. Meanwhile, sift together the flour and baking powder into a mixing bowl. Set aside.

In a large bowl, combine the butter and sugar. Using a hand-held mixer set on medium speed, beat the ingredients until the mixture is very fluffy, light, and pale in color, 6 to 8 minutes. Continuing to beat on medium speed, add the eggs, one at a time, beating well after each addition and scraping down the sides of the bowl with a rubber spatula. Beat in the vanilla and lemon zest. Reduce the speed to low and add the flour mixture, one half at a time, beating well after each addition until thoroughly incorporated. The batter will not be stiff, but will hold the trail of the beaters.

Pour about one third of the batter into a small bowl. Using a wire whisk, quickly whisk 3 to 4 tablespoons of the batter in the small bowl into the warm chocolate, then whisk the chocolate mixture into the small bowl of batter.

Pour about half of the "white batter" into the prepared pan. Pour all of the "chocolate batter" over the layer of white batter. Do not worry if the chocolate layer is not evenly distributed. Pour the remaining white batter over the chocolate layer and shake the pan back and forth to level the top. The pan should only be two-thirds to three-fourths full. Draw a table knife through the batter in a zigzag pattern to marbleize it.

Bake in the preheated oven until the top springs back when touched and a toothpick inserted in the deepest part of the cake comes out dry, 40 to 50 minutes. Remove to a wire rack to cool in the pan for 10 minutes, then invert onto the rack, lift off the pan, and cool completely. The cake will keep, covered, at room temperature for 3 or 4 days.

PAN D'ANGELI AL LIMONE
Lemon Pound Cake

◆

MAKES 2 LOAF CAKES OR ONE 10-INCH RING CAKE; SERVES 16

Unsalted butter and unbleached all-purpose flour for pan(s)

1 pound unsalted butter, at room temperature

2¼ cups sugar

10 eggs

Grated zest of 1 lemon

2 tablespoons fresh lemon juice

4 cups sifted unbleached all-purpose flour

3 ounces white chocolate

Pan d'angeli *is the name of a common Italian cake mix. I remember my mother sending me to the store for the blue package with an angel on it. Inside was a blend of cornstarch, baking powder, and vanilla — the essence of a cake — to which she added eggs, flour, and butter to make a classic yellow* torta.

This recipe, which makes an equally appealing sunny-colored cake, can be successfully halved and then baked in a single loaf pan.

Preheat an oven to 350 degrees F. Using butter, grease a 10-by-4-inch tube pan with a 3-quart capacity or two 8½-by-4½-by-2½-inch loaf pans. Cut out parchment paper to fit the pan bottom(s) precisely and slip into place. Grease the paper and the sides and then dust the sides and paper with flour.

In a large bowl combine the butter and sugar. Using a hand-held mixer set on medium speed, beat the ingredients until the mixture is very fluffy, light, and pale in color, 8 to 10 minutes. Continuing to beat on medium speed, add the eggs, two at a time, beating well after each addition and scraping down the sides of the bowl with a rubber spatula. Beat in the lemon zest and juice. Reduce the speed to low and add the flour, one third at a time, mixing only until incorporated and scraping down the bowl after each addition. The batter will be thick but not stiff.

Pour the batter into the prepared pan(s) and shake the pan(s) back and forth to level it. Cover loosely with aluminum foil and place in the bottom third of the preheated oven. Bake the loaves for 20 minutes or the round cake for 30 minutes. Remove the foil and continue baking until a wooden toothpick inserted in the deepest part of the cake comes out dry and the top has formed a light crust, 60 to 75 minutes for the loaves and about 1¾ hours for the round cake. Remove to a wire rack and cool in the pan(s) for 10 minutes. Invert onto the rack, lift off the pan(s), and peel off the paper. Let cool completely.

Using a vegetable peeler, shave white chocolate curls over the top of the cake(s). To serve, cut into thin slices, letting the curls tumble down the cut sides. To store, wrap well and keep at room temperature for up to 5 days; top with the chocolate curls just before serving.

BIGNÈ

Pastry Puffs Filled with Pastry Cream

◆

Unsalted butter for
baking sheets
(optional)

1 cup water

¼ pound (1 stick)
unsalted butter

½ teaspoon salt

1 teaspoon sugar

1 cup unbleached bread
flour

5 eggs

1 recipe Crema
Pasticceria
(opposite)

⅓ cup powdered sugar

Milanese bakers place trays of pastry cream—filled bignè in their front windows to attract fans of these Italian-style French cream puffs. Passersby turn in to pick up one or two of the powdered sugar—topped dolci, which are sometimes nestled in individual paper cups for easy portage, to savor as they stroll along the street.

Preheat an oven to 450 degrees F. Line 2 baking sheets with parchment paper or grease them with butter.

In a 2-quart saucepan over high heat, combine the water, butter, salt, and sugar. Bring the mixture to a boil, stir to distribute the butter evenly, and remove from the heat. Add the flour all at once and stir it in with a wooden spoon. Return the pan to medium heat and continue stirring vigorously until no lumps of flour remain and the mixture comes away cleanly from the sides of the pan, about 2 minutes.

Transfer the dough to a mixing bowl. Using a hand-held mixer set on low speed, beat in the eggs, one at a time, beating well after each addition. After the third egg is added, scrape down the bowl sides and the beaters with a rubber spatula. Continue adding the remaining eggs in the same manner. After the last addition, scrape the bowl and beaters again and beat briefly to combine with the dough.

Spoon the dough into a pastry bag fitted with a No. 6 plain tip. Pipe out mounds about 1¼ inches in diameter and 1 inch apart onto the prepared sheets. Place the baking sheets in the preheated oven and immediately reduce the oven temperature to 425 degrees F. Bake for 25 minutes, reduce the oven temperature to 375 degrees F, and continue baking until golden brown, 15 to 20 minutes longer. To test for doneness, break open one of the puffs. If the center is dry, it is ready; if it looks doughy, return the baking sheets to the oven for a few more minutes. Cool completely on baking sheets before filling.

Prepare the crema pasticceria and chill well.

Slice the cooled puffs in half crosswise and spoon a small amount of the chilled cream into the bottom half of each one. Replace the tops and arrange on a platter. Just before serving sieve the powdered sugar over the top of the filled puffs. If not serving immediately, cover and refrigerate for up to 4 hours.

CREMA PASTICCERIA
Pastry Cream

◆

Here is a smooth, rich pastry cream that can be used both to fill bignè (opposite) and to spread over flaky pastry shells for fresh fruit crostate (page 176). Always keep this cream — or any sweet that includes it — refrigerated until serving time.

⅓ cup sugar

¼ cup unbleached all-purpose flour

2 tablespoons cornstarch

2 eggs

1 lemon

2 cups milk

1 vanilla bean, or 1 teaspoon vanilla extract

7 tablespoons unsalted butter, at room temperature

Sift together the sugar, flour, and cornstarch into a mixing bowl. Add the eggs. Using a hand-held mixer set on low speed, beat until there are no lumps and the mixture is thick and pale yellow, about 2 minutes. Set aside.

Using a vegetable peeler, remove 5 lengthwise strips of zest from the lemon. Be sure to remove only the yellow portion of the peel, leaving the bitter white pith behind.

In a 1½-quart saucepan over high heat, bring the milk, lemon zest strips, and vanilla bean, if using, to a simmer. Slowly pour the egg mixture into the simmering milk while stirring constantly with a wire whisk. Reduce the heat to medium-high and stir with a wooden spoon until the mixture thickens and coats the back of the spoon, 3 to 5 minutes.

At the appearance of the first bubble on the surface, remove the pan from the heat. Do not allow the pastry cream to boil or it will overcook and become granular. Strain the pastry cream through a fine-mesh sieve into a clean bowl. Stir in the butter, 1 tablespoon at a time, and then the vanilla extract, if using.

Cover the bowl with plastic wrap, pressing the wrap directly onto the surface of the cream so that the cream does not form a skin. Refrigerate until well chilled before using. The cream will keep in the refrigerator for up to 3 days.

◆   ◆   ◆

PANFORTE
Fruitcake of Siena

◆

MAKES ONE 8 1/2-INCH CAKE; SERVES 12 TO 14

The Sienese have been making panforte since medieval times. Laced with spices, nuts, candied fruits, sugar, and a touch of white pepper, it plays the same role at Christmas in Tuscany that fruitcake does in the United States. If you should go to Siena, look for panforte's most respected purveyor, the venerable Nannini, with two shops in the city center.

Because of its richness and intense flavor — it is almost like a candy — panforte should be cut into small wedges for serving. A glass of Asti Spumante, usually dry for the men and sweet for the women, traditionally is offered with the cake.

Preheat an oven to 350 degrees F. Grease an 8-inch-round cake pan with butter. Cut out a round of parchment paper to fit the pan bottom precisely and slip the paper into the pan. Set aside.

Spread the hazelnuts and almonds in a shallow baking pan and place them in the preheated oven until they are lightly toasted, about 10 minutes. Remove from the oven and set aside to cool. Lower the oven temperature to 300 degrees F.

In a large mixing bowl, combine the candied fruits, all of the spices, and the flour and stir together with a wooden spoon. Add the cooled nuts and stir to coat thoroughly with the flour mixture. Set aside.

In a small, heavy saucepan, stir together the granulated sugar and honey and then bring to a boil. Cook the mixture until it registers 250 degrees F on a candy thermometer (hard-ball stage) or a small bit forms a hard ball when pressed between fingertips in ice water. Immediately pour the sugar syrup into the dry ingredients and stir until all the ingredients are well coated.

Pour the batter into the prepared pan. Lightly dampen your hands and press the mixture evenly and firmly into the pan. The cake should be about 1 inch thick. Bake in the preheated oven for 1 hour. The cake will seem underdone at this point, but it will harden as it cools. Cool completely in the pan and then invert onto a platter. Sieve the powdered sugar over the top just before serving. Store in an airtight container at room temperature for up to 2 weeks.

Unsalted butter for cake pan

1½ cups whole raw hazelnuts, roughly chopped

⅔ cup whole raw almonds, roughly chopped

1¾ cups diced mixed candied fruits

¾ teaspoon ground cinnamon

¼ teaspoon ground allspice

¼ teaspoon freshly grated nutmeg

¼ teaspoon ground coriander

⅛ teaspoon ground white pepper

½ cup unbleached all-purpose flour

½ cup granulated sugar

⅔ cup honey

¼ cup powdered sugar

CROSTATA DI MELE
Apple Tart

A visit to Milan is not complete without a visit to Gastronomia Peck, a food emporium to rival the world's best. In addition to mountains of parmigiano-reggiano, chains of salsicce, and seemingly every other wonderful Italian foodstuff imaginable, Peck sells some of the most beautiful fresh fruit tarts on this earth — raspberry, blackberry, plum, peach, apricot, pineapple, kiwi. Many of the most tantalizing creations combine seasonal fruits in colorful patterns.

MAKES ONE 10-INCH TART; SERVES 8 TO 10

My Uncle Ottorino has one of the largest apple orchards in the countryside near Brescia. He loads bushels of Red Delicious apples for market, but always sets aside some of his flavorful fruits for baking into delicious tarts.

You can use any good-quality thick commercial applesauce or your own homemade applesauce as a bed for the fruit slices. The cinnamon should be added to the applesauce only if does not already have a pleasingly fragrant flavor. The apricot glaze, which gives the apples an appealing luster and prevents the fruit from drying out, can be brushed atop other fruit tarts as well. The tart will keep at room temperature for twenty-four hours.

Prepare the pastry dough and chill it for at least 1 hour. Preheat an oven to 350 degrees F.

On a lightly floured board, roll out the dough into a 12½-inch round about ³⁄₁₆ inch thick. Loosely roll the pastry around the pin. Position the pin atop a 10-inch tart pan with ¾-inch fluted sides and a removable bottom and unroll the pastry. Gently press the pastry onto the bottom and sides of the pan. Avoid stretching the dough or it may shrink during baking. Trim off the pastry even with the pan rim and slip the lined tart pan into the freezer until the pastry is just firm to the touch, 10 to 15 minutes.

Cut out a round of aluminum foil about 15 inches in diameter and line the tart shell with it. Fill with pie weights. Bake in the preheated oven until the dough is set and no longer shiny, 12 to 15 minutes. Remove the weights and foil carefully and continue to bake the shell until it just begins to color, about 5 minutes longer. Remove to a wire rack and let cool completely before filling.

Peel, halve, and core the apples. Thinly slice the halves crosswise. Mix the cinnamon, if using, into the applesauce, and spread the applesauce over the bottom of the cooled shell. Arrange the apple slices in overlapping concentric circles on top of the applesauce, placing the slices at right angles to the edge of the crust. Brush the apples evenly with the beaten egg (you may not need all of the egg).

Bake in the preheated oven until the crust is brown and the edges of the apples begin to brown, 25 to 30 minutes. Remove to a wire rack to cool completely.

To make the apricot glaze, in a small saucepan combine the preserves and lemon juice and bring to a boil. Strain through a fine-mesh sieve. You should have about ⅓ cup. (A 10-inch tart will need about ¼ cup glaze.) While still hot, brush a very thin coating of the glaze over the apples (see Note). Let cool, then remove the tart from the pan just before serving.

NOTE   Once the apricot glaze has been strained, it can be stored, covered, in the refrigerator for up to 2 weeks. Just before using, return to a boil, whisking constantly. If the glaze becomes too thick to brush on thinly, whisk in a little water.

½ recipe Pasta Frolla dough (page 151)

Unbleached all-purpose flour for work surface

2 or 3 large tart apples, such as pippin or Granny Smith

Pinch of ground cinnamon (optional)

¾ cup thick applesauce

1 egg, lightly beaten

For the apricot glaze:

½ cup apricot preserves

2 tablespoons fresh lemon juice

♦   ♦   ♦

CROSTATA DI FRUTTA FRESCA
Fresh Fruit Tart

MAKES ONE 10-INCH TART; SERVES 8 TO 10

½ *recipe* Pasta Frolla
dough *(page 151)*

¾ *to 1 cup* Crema
Pasticceria *(page 171)*

*Unbleached all-purpose
flour for work
surface*

2 *to 3 cups prepared
fresh fruit (see
introduction)*

¼ *cup apricot glaze (see
Crostata di Mele,
page 174)*

This tart can be made with any berry or sliced, fleshy fresh fruit that will not turn brown when peeled and exposed to the air. Whole raspberries, blackberries, and grapes; whole, halved, or sliced strawberries (depending upon their size); and peeled and sliced kiwifruits and mangoes are all good choices, either alone or in combination. Serve the tart within twenty-four hours of preparing it. If you prefer to make the tart without the apricot glaze, bake the tart shell and ready the fruit and cream in advance, then assemble the crostata *just before serving.*

Prepare the pastry dough and chill for at least 1 hour. Prepare the *crema pasticceria* and refrigerate until well chilled.

On a lightly floured work surface roll out the dough into a 12½-inch round about ³⁄₁₆ inch thick. Loosely roll the pastry around the pin. Position the pin atop a 10-inch tart pan with ¾-inch fluted sides and a removable bottom and unroll the pastry. Gently press the pastry onto the bottom and sides of the pan. Avoid stretching the dough or it may shrink during baking. Trim off the pastry even with the pan rim and slip the lined tart pan into the freezer until the pastry is firm to the touch, 10 to 15 minutes.

Cut out a round of aluminum foil about 15 inches in diameter and line the tart shell with it. Fill with pie weights. Bake in the preheated oven until the dough is set and no longer shiny, 12 to 15 minutes. Remove the weights and foil carefully and continue to bake the shell until golden brown and fully cooked, 12 to 15 minutes longer. Remove to a wire rack and let cool completely before filling.

Remove the tart ring, leaving the baked shell resting on the bottom. Spread a ¼-inch-thick layer of the chilled pastry cream over the bottom of the shell. Arrange the fruit on the cream in concentric circles, placing the pieces close together so that all of the cream is covered. If using sliced fruit, overlap the slices slightly.

Prepare the apricot glaze. Brush a thin layer of the hot glaze over the fruit. Cover and refrigerate until serving time. Remove from the pan bottom just before serving.

TORTA DI RICOTTA
Ricotta Tart

◆

MAKES ONE 8-INCH TART; SERVES 6 TO 8

In *Italy mild, fresh ricotta is commonly packed into a mold with a basketweave pattern that remains on the surface of the unmolded cheese. Sometimes the rich, soft cheese appears for dessert with just a topping of ground chocolate or coffee. Sicilians mix ricotta with chocolate bits, sugar, and zuccata (melon preserves) and then combine it with delicate sponge cake to make* cassata siciliana, *an extraordinary* dolce *that takes its name from the Arabic-originated terra-cotta mold, or qas' ah, in which it is assembled. A similar ricotta mixture forms the filling for yet another Sicilian classic, crisp* cannoli *tubes, and for the island's* cassateddi, *small deep-fried turnovers that are sprinkled with a dusting of cinnamon and sugar while still warm.*

In this tart, which recalls a popular Roman dessert, lightly sweetened fresh ricotta is flavored with orange zest and vanilla and then enclosed in a flaky pastry package.

◆　◆　◆

RICOTTA

◆

Although today Italian cheese makers sometimes add milk when making ricotta, traditionally this popular cheese was made from the whey left over from making other cheeses, most commonly sheep's milk pecorino in Lazio, Sardinia, Sicily, Umbria, and Tuscany or cow's milk cheeses in Piedmont. The sheep's milk versions are tangier than cow's milk ricotta, and when made with only the whey, have a slightly granular texture. Italians also make a salted ricotta and a dried ricotta they age for grating; Sicilians in particular excel at these mature cheeses.

To make the dough, in a mixing bowl combine the whole egg, egg yolk, milk, and vanilla and lightly beat together with a fork. Set aside.

In a large mixing bowl, stir together the flour, sugar, baking powder, and salt. Add the butter and, using a hand-held mixer set on low speed, beat until the mixture is crumbly and forms pea-sized balls. Add the egg mixture to the flour mixture and beat on low speed until a rough, shaggy mass forms.

Lightly dust your hands with flour and knead the dough in the bowl until all the ingredients are well incorporated and the dough is smooth, 1 to 2 minutes. Divide the dough into two portions, one portion twice as large as the other. Wrap each portion tightly and chill them for 30 minutes.

Grease an 8-inch springform pan with 2-inch sides with butter. On a lightly floured work surface, roll out the larger piece of dough into a 12-inch round about 3/16 inch thick. Loosely roll the pastry around the pin, place the pin on top of the prepared pan, and unroll the pastry. Gently press the pastry onto the bottom and sides of the pan. Avoid stretching the dough or it may shrink during baking. Chill the pastry shell while you prepare the filling.

Preheat an oven to 350 degrees F.

To make the filling, in a mixing bowl combine the ricotta, sugar, vanilla, egg yolk, orange zest, and cream. Using a hand-held mixer set on medium speed, beat the ingredients until the mixture is smooth and fluffy, about 2 minutes. Pour the filling into the pastry-lined pan and level the top with a spatula.

Using a sharp knife trim the pastry so that it reaches 1/2 inch above the level of the filling, then fold the 1/2-inch edge inward so that it rests on top of the filling. On a lightly floured work surface, roll out the remaining dough portion into a round 1/8 inch thick. Cut out an 8-inch round. Pick up the pastry round and rest it directly on top of the filling. Any remaining dough can be gathered up, rolled out 1/8 inch thick, and then cut into decorative shapes such as leaves, stars, or half-moons and arranged on top of the tart. To attach the decorations, brush the bottom of each cutout with a little water and then place the cutout on the top crust.

Bake the *torta* in the preheated oven until golden brown, about 1 hour. Remove from the oven to a wire rack and let cool completely in the pan. Unclasp and remove the pan sides. Using a spatula loosen the *torta* from the pan bottom and slide it onto a serving plate. Store at room temperature for up to 4 hours.

For the pastry dough:

1 whole egg

1 egg yolk

2 teaspoons milk

1/2 teaspoon vanilla extract

2 cups unbleached all-purpose flour

1/2 cup sugar

1 tablespoon baking powder

1/8 teaspoon salt

1/4 pound (1 stick) plus 1 tablespoon unsalted butter, at room temperature

Additional flour for hands and work surface

Additional butter for springform pan

For the ricotta filling:

1 3/4 cups (about 15 ounces) ricotta cheese

2 tablespoons sugar

1/2 teaspoon vanilla extract

1 egg yolk

1 1/2 teaspoons freshly grated orange zest

2 tablespoons whipping cream

TORTA PRIMAVERA

Yellow Cake with Raisins and Jam

Torta Margherita, *a simple yellow cake dusted with powdered sugar, is a traditional sweet of the Easter season. This* torta, *with its pastry crust and thin layers of apricot jam and raisins, is an elaboration of the Margherita. At Il Fornaio we add out-of-season apples to the top.*

Prepare the pastry dough, divide it in half, and chill both portions for at least 1 hour.

On a lightly floured work surface, roll out half of the dough into a 12½-inch round about ³⁄₁₆ inch thick. Loosely roll the pastry around the pin. Position the pin atop a 10-inch tart pan with ¾-inch fluted sides and a removable bottom and unroll the pastry. Gently press the pastry onto the bottom and sides of the pan. Avoid stretching the dough or it may shrink during baking. Trim off the pastry even with the pan rim.

Spread the apricot jam evenly over the bottom of the pastry and scatter the raisins over the jam. Refrigerate the tart shell while you make the cake batter.

Preheat an oven to 350 degrees F. To make the cake, sift together the flour and baking powder into a mixing bowl. Set aside. In a large mixing bowl, combine the butter and sugar. Using a hand-held mixer set on medium speed, beat the ingredients until the mixture is very fluffy, light, and pale in color, 6 to 8 minutes. Continuing to beat on medium speed, add the egg yolks, one at a time, and then the eggs, beating well after each addition. Beat in the vanilla and orange zest. Throughout the mixing process, stop and scrape down the bowl sides several times to make sure all the ingredients are well incorporated. Reduce the speed to low and add the flour mixture, one half at a time, and beat until thoroughly incorporated. The batter will be very thick.

Pour the batter into the prepared tart shell. Using a spatula, spread and smooth the batter so that it mounds slightly in the center.

Peel, halve, and core the apples and then cut them lengthwise into slices ³⁄₈-inch thick. Starting near the rim of the tart pan, arrange the apple slices in concentric circles, overlapping them slightly and covering the entire surface of the cake.

Bake the *torta* in the preheated oven until the top is golden brown and a toothpick inserted in the center comes out dry, 45 to 55 minutes. Remove to a wire rack and let the cake cool for about 15 minutes. Then remove from the tart pan and let cool completely.

To finish the *torta*, prepare the apricot glaze and brush the hot glaze over the apples. Cover and store at room temperature for up to 3 days.

---

1 recipe Pasta Frolla dough (page 151)

Unbleached all-purpose flour for work surface

5 tablespoons apricot jam

½ cup golden raisins

For the cake:

1 cup cake flour

1 teaspoon baking powder

6 tablespoons (¾ stick) unsalted butter, at room temperature

½ cup sugar

2 egg yolks

2 whole eggs

½ teaspoon vanilla extract

½ tablespoon freshly grated orange zest

2 large tart apples, such as pippin or Granny Smith

¼ cup apricot glaze (see Crostata di Mele, page 174)

TORTA DI LIMONE E MERINGA
Lemon Meringue Tart

◆

MAKES ONE 10-INCH TART; SERVES 10

Lemons have a long history in Italy, as is proven in their depiction by Pompeiian mosaic makers and painters. In those days these precious citrus fruits were imported, very rare, and, of course, very costly. By the eighth century the Moors had established lemon cultivation in Sicily. The Sicilians no doubt began concocting their famed pale yellow granita di limone *soon after, as an antidote to the relentless heat of the island's summers.*

Italians make wonderful lemon tarts. They also bake individual crisp meringues, which we call spumiglia *in my hometown and like to dip in chocolate. But I have never seen a lemon meringue tart in Italy. This is Il Fornaio's answer to the craving for the old-fashioned — and beloved — American pie.*

◆   ◆   ◆

Prepare the pastry dough and chill it for at least 1 hour. Preheat an oven to 375 degrees F.

On a lightly floured work surface, roll out the dough into a 12½-inch round about ³⁄₁₆ inch thick. Loosely roll the pastry around the pin. Position the pin atop a 10-inch tart pan with ¾-inch fluted sides and a removable bottom and unroll the pastry. Gently press the pastry onto the bottom and sides of the pan. Avoid stretching the dough or it may shrink during baking. Trim off the pastry even with the pan rim and slip the lined tart pan into the freezer until the pastry is just firm to the touch, 10 to 15 minutes.

Cut out a round of aluminum foil about 15 inches in diameter and line the tart shell with it. Fill with pie weights. Bake in the preheated oven until the dough is set and no longer shiny, 12 to 15 minutes. Remove the weights and foil carefully and continue to bake the shell until it is light brown, 5 to 7 minutes longer. Remove to a wire rack and let cool completely before filling.

While the tart shell is cooling, prepare the lemon filling. In a mixing bowl, combine the eggs and sugar. Using a hand-held mixer set on medium speed, beat the ingredients until the mixture is very fluffy, light, pale in color, and trails from the beaters, 6 to 8 minutes. Continuing to beat on medium speed, beat in the cream, lemon juice, and zest until thoroughly incorporated.

Pour the filling into the cooled tart shell. (This step is easiest to do if the tart shell is already on the oven rack; transporting the filled tart shell to the oven rack may result in spillage.)

Bake the filled tart shell until the center is just set, 18 to 20 minutes. The filling should jiggle slightly but not appear liquid. Remove from the oven to a wire rack and let cool completely.

Increase the oven temperature to 450 degrees F. To prepare the meringue topping, place the egg whites, cream of tartar, and sugar in a grease-free glass or ceramic bowl (fat prevents the egg whites from beating properly). Rest the bowl in a pan above gently boiling water, much like a double boiler. Whisking lightly with a wire whisk to keep the egg whites from cooking along the edges of the bowl, heat the mixture until it is hot to the touch and feels slick. Transfer the egg-white mixture to a second grease-free glass or ceramic bowl and beat on high speed until the egg white mixture holds stiff peaks.

Spoon the egg whites into a pastry bag fitted with a No. 7 star tip and pipe them onto the top of the tart, making sure the filling is completely covered. Alternatively, spread the mixture on with a rubber spatula. Place the tart back in the oven until the meringue is lightly browned. This takes only a few minutes, so watch the tart carefully. You may want to turn the tart as it bakes, to compensate for any area of the oven that may be hotter than the rest. Remove to a wire rack and let cool completely before removing from the pan. Store at room temperature for up to 4 hours.

½ recipe Pasta Frolla dough (page 151)

Unbleached all-purpose flour for work surface

For the lemon filling:

5 eggs

9 tablespoons sugar

3 tablespoons whipping cream

⅔ cup fresh lemon juice

1 teaspoon freshly grated lemon zest

For the meringue topping:

1 cup egg whites (8 eggs)

⅛ teaspoon cream of tartar

1½ cups sugar

INDEX

TABLE OF EQUIVALENTS

The exact equivalents in the following tables have been rounded for convenience.

US/UK

oz = ounce

lb = pound

in = inch

ft = foot

tbl = tablespoon

fl oz = fluid ounce

qt = quart

Metric

g = gram

kg = kilogram

mm = millimeter

cm = centimeter

ml = milliliter

l = liter

WEIGHTS

US/UK	Metric
I oz	30 g
2 oz	60 g
3 oz	90 g
4 oz (¼ lb)	125 g
5 oz (⅓ lb)	155 g
6 oz	185 g
7 oz	220 g
8 oz (½ lb)	250 g
10 oz	315 g
12 oz (¾ lb)	375 g
14 oz	440 g
16 oz (I lb)	500 g
I½ lb	750 g
2 lb	I kg
3 lb	1.5 kg

OVEN TEMPERATURES

Fahrenheit	Celsius	Gas
250	120	½
275	140	I
300	150	2
325	160	3
350	180	4
375	190	5
400	200	6
425	220	7
450	230	8
475	240	9
500	260	10

LIQUIDS

US	Metric	UK
2 tbl	30 ml	I fl oz
¼ cup	60 ml	2 fl oz
⅓ cup	80 ml	3 fl oz
½ cup	125 ml	4 fl oz
⅔ cup	160 ml	5 fl oz
¾ cup	180 ml	6 fl oz
I cup	250 ml	8 fl oz
I½ cups	375 ml	12 fl oz
2 cups	500 ml	16 fl oz
4 cups/I qt	I l	32 fl oz

LENGTH MEASURES

⅛ in	3 mm
¼ in	6 mm
½ in	12 mm
I in	2.5 cm
2 in	5 cm
3 in	7.5 cm
4 in	10 cm
5 in	13 cm
6 in	15 cm
7 in	18 cm
8 in	20 cm
9 in	23 cm
10 in	25 cm
II in	28 cm
12 in/I ft	30 cm

Equivalents for Commonly Used Ingredients

All-Purpose (Plain) Flour / Dried Bread Crumbs / Chopped Nuts

¼ cup	I oz	30 g
⅓ cup	1½ oz	45 g
½ cup	2 oz	60 g
¾ cup	3 oz	90 g
I cup	4 oz	125 g
1½ cups	6 oz	185 g
2 cups	8 oz	250 g

Whole-Wheat (Wholemeal) Flour

3 tbl	I oz	30 g
½ cup	2 oz	60 g
⅔ cup	3 oz	90 g
I cup	4 oz	125 g
1¼ cups	5 oz	155 g
1⅔ cups	7 oz	210 g
1¾ cups	8 oz	250 g

Brown Sugar

¼ cup	1½ oz	45 g
½ cup	3 oz	90 g
¾ cup	4 oz	125 g
I cup	5½ oz	170 g
1½ cups	8 oz	250 g
2 cups	10 oz	315 g

White Sugar

¼ cup	2 oz	60 g
⅓ cup	3 oz	90 g
½ cup	4 oz	125 g
¾ cup	6 oz	185 g
I cup	8 oz	250 g
1½ cups	12 oz	375 g
2 cups	I lb	500 g

Raisins / Currants / Semolina

¼ cup	I oz	30 g
⅓ cup	2 oz	60 g
½ cup	3 oz	90 g
¾ cup	4 oz	125 g
I cup	5 oz	155 g

Long-Grain Rice / Cornmeal

⅓ cup	2 oz	60 g
½ cup	2½ oz	75 g
¾ cup	4 oz	125 g
I cup	5 oz	155 g
1½ cups	8 oz	250 g

Dried Beans

¼ cup	1½ oz	45 g
⅓ cup	2 oz	60 g
½ cup	3 oz	90 g
¾ cup	5 oz	155 g
1 cup	6 oz	185 g
1¼ cups	8 oz	250 g
1½ cups	12 oz	375 g

Rolled Oats

⅓ cup	1 oz	30 g
⅔ cup	2 oz	60 g
1 cup	3 oz	90 g
1½ cups	4 oz	125 g
2 cups	5 oz	155 g

Jam/Honey

2 tbl	2 oz	60 g
¼ cup	3 oz	90 g
½ cup	5 oz	155 g
¾ cup	8 oz	250 g
1 cup	11 oz	345 g

Grated Parmesan/Romano Cheese

¼ cup	1 oz	30 g
½ cup	2 oz	60 g
¾ cup	3 oz	90 g
1 cup	4 oz	125 g
1⅓ cups	5 oz	155 g
2 cups	7 oz	220 g